Focke-Wulf Fw 190A

Focke-Wulf Fw 190A

An Illustrated History of the Luftwaffe's Legendary Fighter Aircraft

Dietmar Hermann, Ulrich Leverenz, & Eberhard Weber

Duane Reves
Box 295
Bruno, Sk.
S0K 0S0

Schiffer Military History
Atglen, PA

Cover artwork by Steve Ferguson, Colorado Springs, CO.
An interpolation of a photo attributed to 5./JG 1 *Staffelkapitan Leutnant* Rudiger von Kirchmayr. This red nosed A-5 bears the infamous I. *Gruppe Tatzelwurm* emblem readily displayed until late 1943, when the "winged 1" logo inspired by *Kommodore* Walter Oesau would supercede all *gruppe* markings. As for von Krchmayr, he proved to be one of the most able *Tatzelwurm* fighters of this legendary unit. His combat career in the Fw 190 played out predominantly with JG 1, where the majority of his forty-six aerial victories were recorded. Although his count was modest by com-

parison to the legendary *Ritterkreuztrager* serving throughout the *Reichsvertelgung*, few *experten* could match his success against a variety of Allied opponents, including twenty-one four-engined Liberators and Flying Fortresses. As a hunter-leader, his methods were simple: get sun-up, get close.

In the spring of 1945, von Kirchmayr left the ravaged JG 1 as a replacement *Staffelkapitan* for the equally war weary I./JG 11. At the close of hostilities, the veteran *viermot* killer found brief refuge with the outcasts of Galland's JV 44 and his long overdue *Ritterkreuz* citation.

Photo credits:
Herr Leonhardt, Laatzen Aviaton Museum

Drawings: Ulrich Leverenz

Translated from the German by David Johnston
Book Design by Ian Robertson.

Copyright © 2004 by Schiffer Publishing.
Library of Congress Catalog Number: 2003111211

Printed in China.
ISBN: 0-7643-1940-X

This book was originally printed under the title,
Focke-Wulf Fw 190A Die ersten Baureihen by Aviatic Verlag.

For the largest selection of fine reference books on this and related subjects, please visit our website - **www.schifferbooks.com** - or call for a free catalog.

We are interested in hearing from authors with book ideas on related topics.

Published by Schiffer Publishing Ltd.
4880 Lower Valley Road
Atglen, PA 19310
Phone: (610) 593-1777
FAX: (610) 593-2002
E-mail: info@schifferbooks.com.
Visit our web site at: www.schifferbooks.com
Please write for a free catalog.
This book may be purchased from the publisher.
Please include $3.95 postage.
Try your bookstore first.

In Europe, Schiffer books are distributed by:
Bushwood Books
6 Marksbury Avenue
Kew Gardens
Surrey TW9 4JF
England
Phone: 44 (0) 20 8392-8585
FAX: 44 (0) 20 8392-9876
E-mail: info@bushwoodbooks.co.uk.
Free postage in the UK. Europe: air mail at cost.
Try your bookstore first.

Contents

Acknowledgments

We wish to thank the following for their assistance
and kind support in the creation of this book:

Claus Colling of the Flugwerk GmbH
Guenther Leonhardt of the Laatzen Aviation Museum

Foreword

When we began this book project, it was our goal to mark the 60th anniversary of the first flight of the Fw 190. For much of the war, the Messerschmitt Bf 109 and the Focke-Wulf Fw 190 were the standard fighter aircraft of the *Luftwaffe*'s day fighter units. The Focke-Wulf's reputation as one of the great fighter aircraft of all times remains undiminished to this day. This book describes how the development of the Fw 190 began and the technical conditions under it was pursued.

It is also our desire to present high-quality photographs in a large format. Every reader with an interest in historical aviation knows that many publications leave much to be desired in this area.

From the start it was also our idea to complement the history of the Fw 190 with firsthand accounts by people who were there. In our book they tell their stories, from the humblest ferry pilot to the test pilots. Every chapter on the Fw 190 includes at least one account by an eyewitness.

Chief test pilot Dipl. Ing. Hans Sander.

Flugkapitän Hans Sander leaving the cockpit of a Fw 190 A-3, WNr. 410.

During our research we were given the unique opportunity to gain new and interesting details about the Fw 190 from the experiences and recollections of Focke-Wulf's former chief test pilot, Hans Sander. At the time we did not know that this would be our last opportunity to do so.

Hans Sander died on 1 February 2000, the last of the Focke-Wulf test pilots. This book also serves as a memorial to that group of men. For this reason we have added an additional chapter on these test pilots. Hans Sander had the opportunity to read a draft of this chapter, and his personal comments about the Focke-Wulf test pilots form part of the final product.

He will be remembered.

The Focke-Wulf Test Pilots

The construction of aircraft in Germany experienced a major upswing in the mid-1930s. Companies like Heinkel, Dornier and Junkers delivered the first aircraft to the newly-created *Luftwaffe*. The air force's first fighter aircraft was the Heinkel He 51, a biplane. The biplane fighter concept was soon relegated to history, however, as development was pursued to meet the requirement of "ever faster, ever higher". The *Luftwaffe* issued a requirement for a new monoplane fighter with a retractable undercarriage. The manufacturers responded, Arado with the Ar 80, Heinkel with the He 112, Messerschmitt with the Bf 109 and Focke-Wulf with the Fw 159, its first fighter design. Unlike the other designs, the Fw 159 was a parasol monoplane, and its highly-complicated undercarriage retraction mechanism caused problems. The Fw 159's performance was inferior to that of the competing designs and it was soon eliminated from the competition, which was eventually won by the Bf 109.

After the demise of the Fw 159, Focke-Wulf turned its efforts to a new project, the Fw 187, a twin-engined fighter aircraft. Like the Fw 159, the Fw 187 was designed by a team headed by Kurt Tank. Tank, who later became Focke-Wulf's technical director, made the first flight in the Fw 187 V1 in the spring of 1937. The aircraft was a direct competitor of the Bf 110 and possessed a superior performance. Despite the fact that Focke-Wulf was unable to obtain the desired DB 600 engines and was forced to use the less powerful Jumo 210, the Fw 187 proved to be faster than the contemporary versions of the Bf 109 and He 112. Flight testing was con-

Prior to a test flight, test pilot Bernhard Märschel in conversation with Focke-Wulf executive Georg Kohne.

The Fw 187 was an excellent design, with an impressive maximum speed and outstanding aerodynamics. Inexplicably, the Fw 187 never went into production.

ducted by Dipl.Ing. Hans Sander, who joined Focke-Wulf in 1937 to take charge of prototype flight testing. Sander came from the *E-Stelle* engine with GM 1 boost. The planned production version of the aircraft was designated the Fw 190 B, however just three Fw 190 B-0 pre-production and two Fw 190 B-1 production aircraft were built.

Focke-Wulf suffered a great loss with the death of Dipl.Ing. Kurt Mehlhorn, who was shot down while on an industry defense sortie in WNr. 0725 (aircraft number "2"). Mehlhorn abandoned the aircraft, but his parachute failed to open. His death was especially tragic for his fiancée, as they were to have been married that day.

Mehlhorn had been involved in testing the Fw 189 tactical reconnaissance aircraft, the Fw 200 Condor, and the Fw 191. The Fw 191 was developed by Focke-Wulf as part of the "Bomber B Program", which was supposed to produce a successor to the Ju 88 medium bomber. Other competitors were the Junkers Ju 288, which was the favorite, the Dornier Do 317 and the Henschel Hs 130. Chief Engineer Sander said of the downing of Kurt Mehlhorn, "Mehlhorn was my deputy, a good pilot and first-class shot. On his last mission he shot

down three Flying Fortresses in frontal attacks. Low on fuel and ammunition, he requested guidance to the nearest airfield. In the process he probably fell victim to escort fighters."

As the Allies gained air superiority, the test pilots were in danger on the ground as well as in the air. Rolf Mondry, who had been a test pilot with Focke-Wulf since 1943, was seriously wounded in a strafing attack on Langenhagen shortly before the Industry Defense Flights were disbanded in the spring of 1944. He subsequently lost an arm. Werner Kampmeier was rather luckier. During an intercept mission over Hanover his canopy was shot away. Kampmeier made an emergency landing at Hanover-Vahrenwald but survived. On 9 October 1943 Alfred Motsch made an emergency landing on Helgoland after his Fw 190 A (aircraft number "5", WNr. 781) was damaged in combat.

Test pilot Fröbl and *Oberleutnant* of the Reserve Hans Böhnert were both killed flying industry defense missions in March 1944. The loss of such highly-trained test pilots was keenly felt by Focke-Wulf. When the Allies resumed their bombing offensive in February 1944, the *Luftwaffe* command

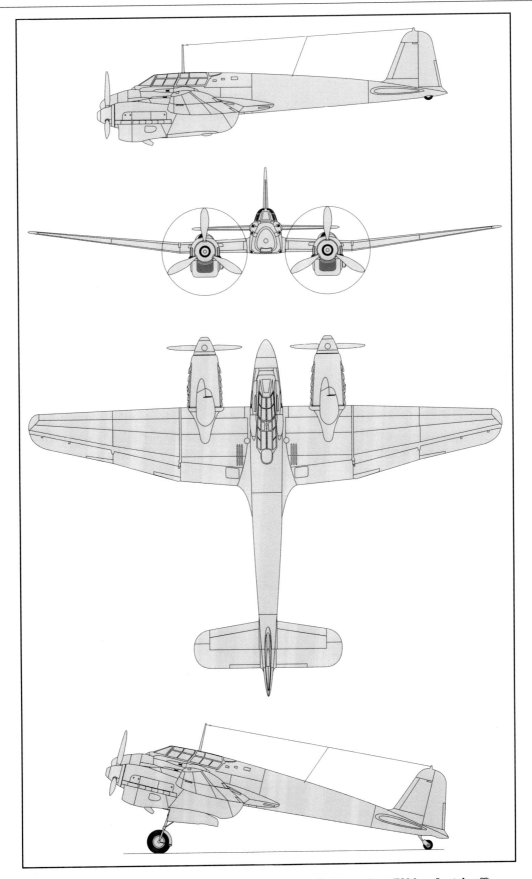

The Fw 187 A Falke, powered by two Jumo 210 G twelve-cylinder engines (730 h.p. for takeoff).

The Fw 187 as a Zerstörer.

apparently recognized the futility of flight-strength missions against escorted bombers. For this and other reasons the Industry Defense Flights were disbanded on 1 March 1944.

In the final two years of the war Focke-Wulf concentrated its efforts on the new Ta 152 H high-altitude fighter and the Ta 154 night fighter. Equipped with a pressurized cockpit, the Ta 152 H was designed to intercept the American B-29 Superfortress, which was expected to appear in the skies over Germany. The Ta 152 was made entirely of wood and was designed to counter the British Mosquito. Both types had to be tested extensively before they could enter service. All did not go smoothly, however, and there were accidents.

The Ta 154 experienced serious problems with its undercarriage, especially the hydraulics. It was discovered that forced landings were extremely risky for the pilot and radio operator as a result of the type's shoulder-wing configuration. In a belly landing the fuselage struck the ground first and disintegrated, as the wooden structure was incapable of absorbing the weight of the entire aircraft. Either the wooden skinning shattered, posing a threat to the crew, or the crew seats were thrown from the fuselage. The initial response was an emergency landing skid, similar to that of the Me 163, while in production aircraft (Ta 154 C) the entire cockpit assembly was to have been made of metal.

The Ta 154 V9 (WNr. 100 009, manufacturer's code TE+FM) was the first aircraft of this type to be lost. The first Ta 154 from the Posen factory, it was delivered in sub-assemblies and assembled in the factory in preparation for later large-scale production. Werner Bartsch assumed responsibility for flight testing. A former fighter pilot, Bartsch had been Adolf Galland's wingman, after later flew Ju 88 bombers on the Eastern Front. He joined Focke-Wulf as a test pilot on 14 August 1942.

On 9 April 1944 the Focke-Wulf factory in Posen was attacked by the American 8th Air Force, seriously affecting Fw 190 production there. A few days later, on 18 April, Werner Bartsch took the Ta 154 V9 into the air on its maiden flight. Bartsch was forced to use the emergency compressed air system to lower the flaps and undercarriage. The flaps, which were not coupled mechanically, did not lower evenly, and Bartsch was unable to keep the wings level. The tips of the right wing and horizontal stabilizer touched the ground first. Bartsch was thrown from the aircraft in his seat. He struck one of the propellers and was seriously injured. Help came too late for Meyer of production control, who was flying in the rear seat. One month later, on 6 May 1944, there was another serious accident. The Ta 154 V8 (WNr. 100 008, manufacturer's code TE+FL) was the first aircraft of the se-

Above: Test pilot Mehlhorn and Kurt Tank. Below: Sitting next to Wallenhorst, chief controller of test flying (center) are Bernhard Märschel and Werner Bartsch (2nd from right and right).

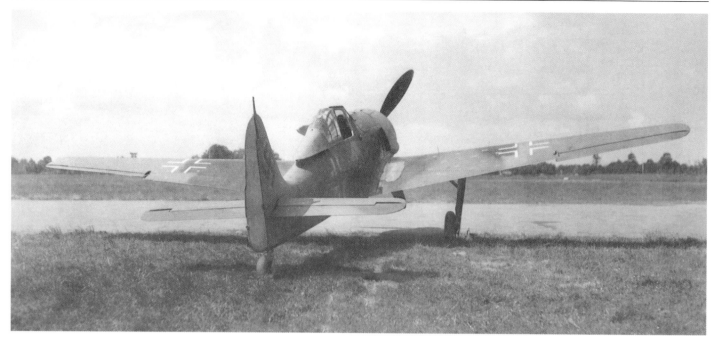

The Fw 190 V47, WNr. 0047, was the prototype for the planned Fw 190 B series.

7. Juni 1940

Antrag
zur Erteilung eines erweiterten Militär-Flugzeugführerscheins

		Geb. Datum	Ort
Leutnant u. Staffelführer	Kurt Tank	24.02.1898	Bromberg
Uffz. u. stellv. Staffelführer	Kurt Mehlhorn	12.06.1912	Jena
Fl.	August Linde	30.06.1912	Bremen
Fl.	Ewald Rohlfs	23.03.1911	Danzig
Fl.	Johann Sander	25.09.1908	Barmen
Fl.	Walter Schorn	21.10.1911	Hilden
Fl.	Hans Schubert	04.01.1902	Spandau
Fl.	Wolfgang Stein	28.05.1902	Berlin
Fl.	Ludwig Vogel	26.05.1909	Stuttgart

Uffz. Hellmut Bischof und Gefr. Hermann Schlegel sind auch Angehörige der Schutzstaffel, aber haben schon einen erw. M.-Fl. F.schein.

K. Tank

Letter from Focke-Wulf to the RLM requesting combat pilot certificates for various pilots in preparation for the formation of the Industry Defense Flight.

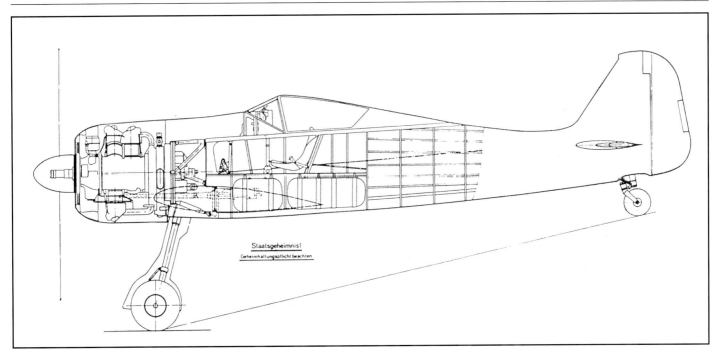

Fw 190 B

ries to be powered by Jumo 213 A engines. During the fifth flight, with pilot Otto and aircraft engineer Rolf Rettig on board, the starboard engine caught fire. The Ta 154 was still at high altitude above the clouds. Otto attempted an emergency landing near Goslar, however the aircraft crashed and both men were thrown out of the cockpit and killed. Luitpold Otto had been a successful bomber pilot, having flown missions over Poland, Holland, Belgium, France and finally Great Britain (in the "Little Blitz"). He was wounded in action,

which left him unable to continue flying bombers. Otto subsequently joined Focke-Wulf as a test pilot on 1 March 1944. Wolf Rettig had been with Focke-Wulf since February 1939, working his way up from fitter to test engineer. He joined the Ta 154 flight test program as an observer, recording flight data. The Ta 154 program's third serious accident, on 13 July 1944, ended in the destruction of the V10, the third prototype equipped with Jumo 213 A engines (WNr. 100 010, manufacturer's code TE+FN). While flying on one engine at

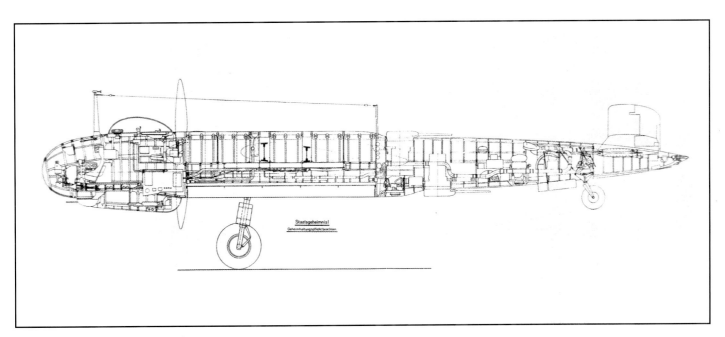

The Fw 191 was another modern design that failed to enter production because of a lack of suitable power plants and indecisiveness on the part of the RLM.

a height of 300 meters, the Jumo 213 A caught fire. With the fire spreading quickly, the pilot was forced to attempt an immediate landing. He managed to put the aircraft down on the ground, however the V10 was completely destroyed by fire. In spite of these accidents, including the loss of two of the four prototypes equipped with the Jumo 213 A, it was believed that a version of the Ta 154 with the improved Jumo 213 E would be able to counter the Mosquito night fighters. Unfortunately for Focke-Wulf, however, the Jumo 213 E engine was not yet available for the Ta 154. Nevertheless, the Ta 154 prototypes powered by the Jumo 213 A displayed an impressive performance. The Ta 154 V10 achieved speeds of 550 km/h at sea level and 661 km/h at 6600 meters.

13 July 1944 was a black day for Focke-Wulf, for a prototype of the Ta 152 H high-altitude fighter was also involved in a serious accident on that day. The prototype for the Ta 152 H series, the Fw 190 V33/U1 (WNr. 0 058, manufacturer's code GH+KW), took off from Adelheide its first flight with the new Jumo 213 E high-altitude engine. The V33 had previously been part of the "*Höhenjäger II*" program. The "*Höhenjäger II*" was an attempt by Focke-Wulf to produce a high-altitude fighter by installing a Daimler Benz DB 603 engine and Hirth TKL 011 turbosupercharger in the airframe

of the Fw 190. The aircraft was also fitted with a new wing, the so-called "Parisian Wing" (produced in France), with a span of 12.3 meters and an area of 20.3 m², plus a pressurized cockpit, as the new engine system had a maximum boost altitude of 11000 meters. The aircraft was subsequently converted at Adelheide to serve as prototype for the Ta 152 H and was redesignated the Fw 190 V33/U1. After its maiden flight, the V33/U1 was supposed to be flown to Focke-Wulf's test center at Langenhagen. The aircraft developed engine trouble en route, however, and sustained 70% damage in an emergency landing at Vechta. The second serious accident occurred a short time later on 23 August 1944. On that day the experienced test pilot Alfred Thomas took off from Adelheide on a test flight in the Fw 190 V30/U1, the second Ta 152 H prototype. The Fw 190 V30/U1 (WNr. 0055, manufacturer's code GH+KT) had also been involved in Focke-Wulf's "*Höhenjäger II*" program and was later converted to serve as a prototype for the Ta 152 H series. While flying at high altitude, the aircraft's engine caught fire. Thomas attempted to land the V30/U1, however it crashed while on approach and he was killed. There is no information as to the exact cause of the accident. "As we in Langenhagen had no radio contact with him, we knew nothing more," said Hans

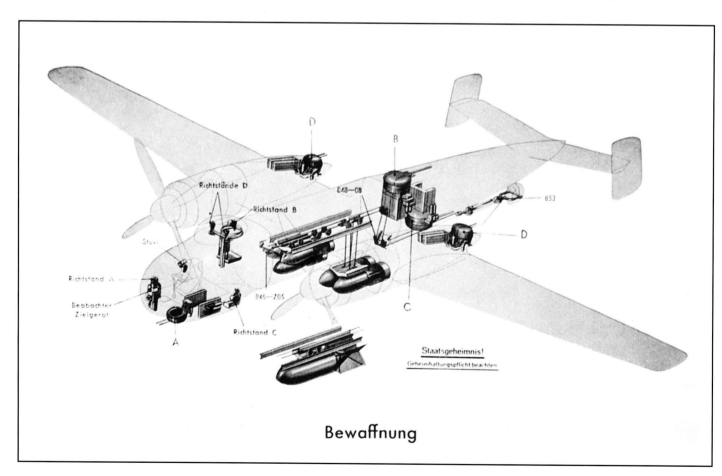

Bewaffnung

Drawing depicting the armament of the twin-engined Fw 191.

Test pilot in the cockpit of a Fw 190 A-2.

Sander. All that is known for certain is that Thomas could have taken to his parachute, but did not do so in an attempt to save the V30/U1. He almost succeeded, but then the aircraft crashed from low altitude. Other Focke-Wulf test pilots survived the war, like Bernhard Märschel and Friedrich Schnier. A former fighter pilot, Bernhard Märschel joined the Focke-Wulf flight test department in 1942. "He was outstanding in determining an aircraft's performance in flight", said Hans Sander. Märschel's final activities with Focke-Wulf were test-flying the latest experimental versions of the Ta 152 H with the Jumo 213 E and the Fw 190 D with the Jumo 213 F. The Jumo 213 E/F represented the apex of piston engine development in Germany. It was equipped with a three-speed, two-stage compressor-supercharger, which allowed it to produce 1,260 h.p. at an altitude of 10700 meters. In the winter of 1944-45 Märschel test-flew the first prototype of the new Ta

152 C fighter at Adelheide. The Ta 152 C was the standard production variant of the Ta 152 and was to have been equipped with the new Daimler Benz DB 603 LA engine producing 2,000 h.p. The DB 603 LA was also supposed to have powered the Ta 152 H and the new Dornier Do 335. Obfw. Friedrich Schnier joined the Focke-Wulf flight testing department when the Ta 154 Test Detachment at Langenhagen was disbanded on 1 August 1944. Schnier had given flight demonstrations in the Ta 154, and on one occasion he succeeded in outturning the prototype of the Bf 109 H, the Bf 109 V54. The name Schnier is also associated with an impressive high-altitude flight in the Ta 152 V29/U1 on 20 January 1945, when he reached an altitude of 13,654 meters.

By 1945 the general situation had made it impossible to conduct structural strength tests on the ground, and load factors had to be determined in the air. Friedrich Schnier carried out several of these potentially dangerous flights.

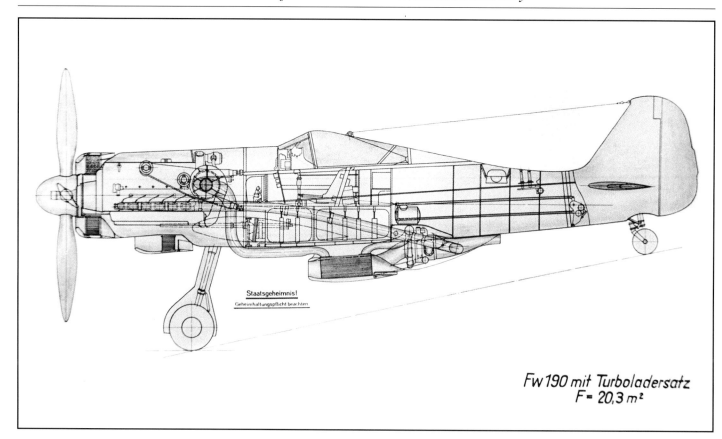

Fw 190 mit Turboladersatz
F = 20,3 m²

Staatsgeheimnis!
Geheimhaltungspflicht beachten

The Höhenjäger 2, powered by a DB 603 engine with exhaust-driven turbosupercharger.

Test flying always included an element of risk. Depicted here are the remains of GH+KU, which overturned on landing. Werner Bartsch survived this accident.

Hptm. Walter Nowotny with Focke-Wulf test pilots. From left to right: Hans Kampmeier, Rolf Mondry, Hptm. Nowotny and Alfred Motsch.

Walter Nowotny in conversation with Focke-Wulf test pilots.

The Fw 190 V53 (WNr. 170003), manufacturer's code DU+JC, powered by the Jumo 213 A.

The V53 in the prototype shop with engine cowlings removed, revealing its Jumo 213 A engine.

Overly hasty engine testing resulted in the loss of the first two examples of the Ta 152 H. Test pilot Alfred Thomas lost his life in GH+KT.

The prototype of the Ta 152 H-0 (Fw 190 V30/U1), manufacturer's code GH+KT. The aircraft's wingspan was 14.44 meters.

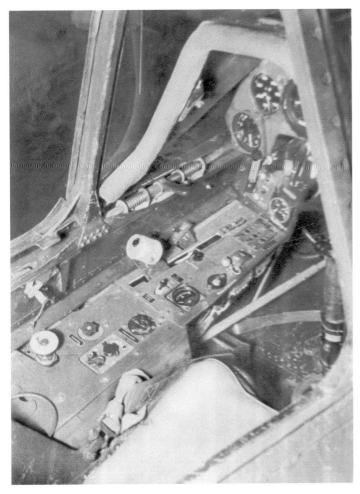

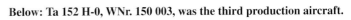

Above and left: Cockpit of the Ta 152 H.

Below: Ta 152 H-0, WNr. 150 003, was the third production aircraft.

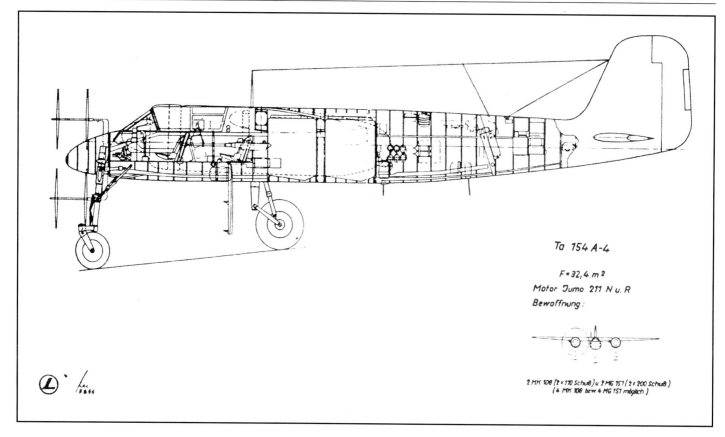

Cutaway drawing of the Ta 154 A-4, dated June 1944.

At 91 years of age, former Chief Test Pilot Hans Sander is the last surviving member of the Focke-Wulf prototype test department. Far too little has been written about this interesting chapter of test flying by Focke-Wulf, which was founded in 1924. The test pilots who risked their lives to bring new aircraft to the point where they could enter production are largely unknown.

Hans Sander never forgot his contemporaries and after the war remained in touch with Rolf Mondry, Werner Bartsch and Hans Kampmeier.

The Focke-Wulf company no longer exists, however aircraft are still being built in Bremen. After the war Focke-Wulf and Weserflug were combined to form the Vereinigten Flugtechnischen Werken, which later fused with MBB and today forms part of the EADS air and space concern.

Development of the Fw 190

In 1937 a design team led by Dipl.Ing. Kurt Tank created a twin-engined high-speed fighter aircraft, the Focke-Wulf Fw 187 *Falke* (Falcon). During development of the Fw 187 Kurt Tank advanced the theory to the RLM that a twin-engined fighter would be more suitable for operations over enemy territory than a single-engined fighter. A twin-engined machine would have the advantage of being able to return to base following the loss of one engine.

This concept was rejected by the RLM. It wanted a twin-engined fighter, but only for the newly created *Zerstörer* (strategic fighter) role. In 1937, while Focke-Wulf was still redesigning the Fw 187 for the *Zerstörer* role, the *Technische Amt* (Technical Office) issued a new specification for a single-engined, single-seat pursuit fighter. Required were:

1. Short production times with design optimized for large-scale production,
2. Maximum reliability through the elimination of liquid cooling,
3. Ease of servicing through good accessibility to the entire engine system and accessories, plus
4. Good protection for the pilot in the main directions of fire.

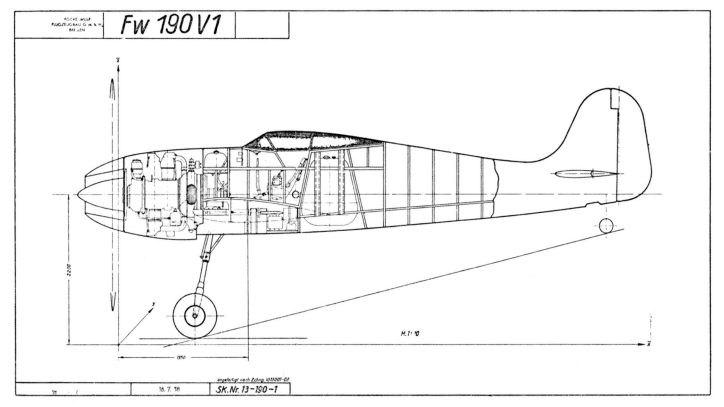

Drawing of the V1 with BMW 139, dated 18 July 1938.

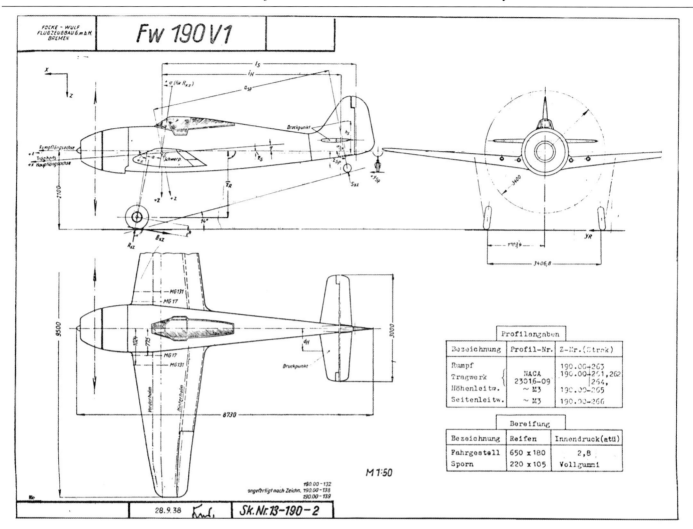

Chief Engineer Rudolf Blaser was responsible for the design of the Fw 190 "*Würger*" (Shrike) from the first prototype to the Ta 152. Born in Switzerland, his career began during the First World War when he worked on large aircraft at the Gothaer Werken. He subsequently worked for AGO in Berlin, AERO in Prague, as an assistant designer for the Swiss Aircraft Works in Thurn, and finally for Albatros in Berlin. Blaser was a department head in the design bureau until Albatros merged with the Focke-Wulf Flugzeugbau GmbH. In 1936 he moved to Bremen, and in 1934 became a German citizen. Blaser was a capable technician with numerous inventions to his credit. He performed brilliantly in his first major assignment in Bremen, designing the Fw 56 *Stösser*. Named chief designer for single-seat aircraft, he was placed in charge of the design team responsible for the new pursuit fighter. Focke-Wulf placed great hopes in this undertaking, for what was at stake was an alternative to the Bf 109, the *Luftwaffe*'s standard fighter, and the successful design would be required in large numbers. Blaser, who had successfully directed work on the Fw 187, was given ten months to complete the project, which had received the RLM designation Fw 190. He spared neither himself nor his coworkers in his efforts to make the first flight by the deadline of 1 June 1939. Although the prototype's flight characteristics were deemed satisfactory from the outset, the planned armament installation was not satisfactory. The access panels for the MG 17 machine-guns were located in the area of the wing roots and were held in place by screws, forming part of the stressed skin structure. The installation of guns above the engine cowling, however, would have required a complete redesign of the upper forward fuselage. The weapons system in front of the cockpit was not realized until the adoption of the BMW 801 engine.

Project model. Note that it has three fuselage-mounted weapons and two in the wings.

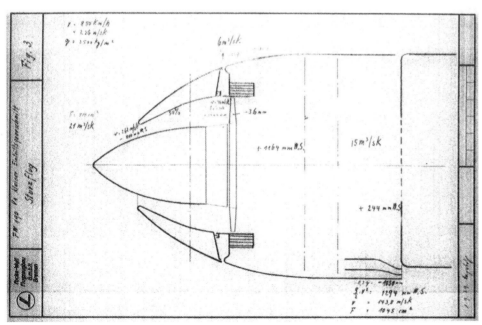

Focke-Wulf developed an innovative double cowling in place of a conventional NACA cowling. This drawing is dated 1 Sept. 1939.

Focke-Wulf subsequently began work anew on a single-engined fighter aircraft. A short time earlier Focke-Wulf's Fw 159 had lost to the Messerschmitt Bf 109 in the competition for a new fighter aircraft for the *Luftwaffe*. Building on its experience with the single-engined Fw 159 and twin-engined Fw 187, the new fighter was designed as a cantilever low-wing monoplane with a retractable undercarriage and air-cooled twin-row radial engine. Kurt Tank's team stressed simplicity and robustness in designing the new fighter.

The experienced engineer Rudolf Blaser was responsible for the detailed design work. From the beginning much emphasis was placed on details in designing the new fighter. The design was kept as simple as possible to allow semi-skilled workers to construct the aircraft quickly and easily. The fuselage, wing and tail section were therefore designed as monocoque structures. The new design differed from the *Luftwaffe*'s standard fighter, the Bf 109, in having an air-cooled radial engine.

The new fighter's wide-track undercarriage also differed from that of the Messerschmitt fighter. One other difference was the fully encapsulated radial engine. Initially Focke-Wulf

received a contract from the RLM to build three prototypes. The RLM also assigned a designation for the new fighter aircraft: Focke-Wulf Fw 190.

The only suitable air-cooled engine available at that time was the BMW 139, which produced 1,500 h.p. for takeoff. The fuselage of the Fw 190 was designed around the shape of the radial engine. Focke-Wulf's design for the engine cowling was innovative. The selected design was a double cowling, which was hoped to provide superior aerodynamics. The forward portion of the double cowling rotated with the propeller, with cooling air entering through a central opening. To minimize the risk associated with this innovative design, Focke-Wulf and BMW conducted trials in a wind tunnel in the hope of eliminating potential cooling problems.

There were also differences of opinion in working out the design. The design of the Fw 190 from the design department headed by Andreas von Faehlmann did not meet with complete approval from Rudolf Blaser. Von Faehlmann had designed a relatively fat fuselage which tapered aft of the engine. Rudi Blaser modified this in a relatively unorthodox fashion, drawing a straight line with a pencil on the design

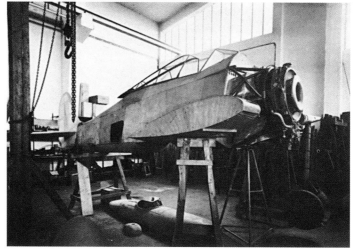

Full-scale mock-up of the single-seat pursuit fighter.

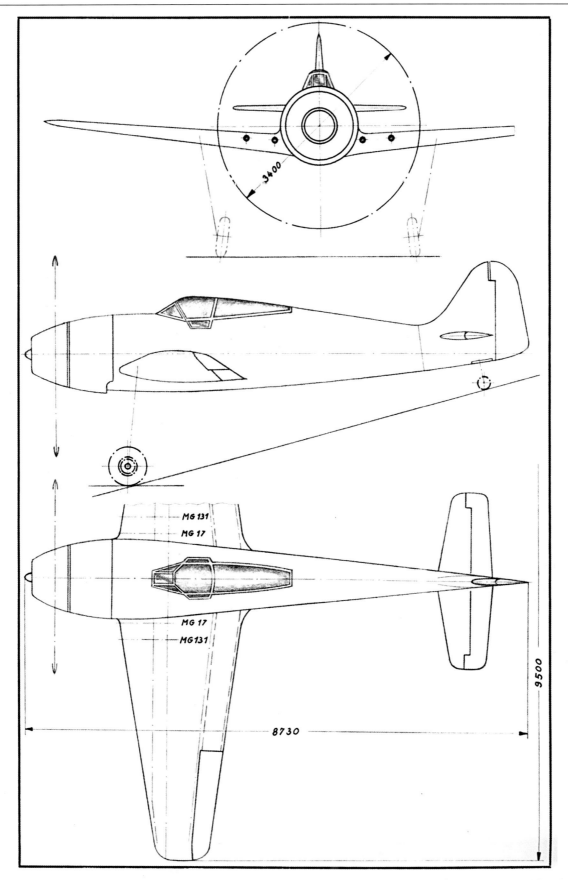

Design for the single-seat pursuit fighter with BMW 139, double cowling and four wing-mounted machine-guns.

Model of the Fw 190 V1. Main spars, control surfaces and skinning panels have been marked on the outer surface of the wooden model.

Technical Description No. 187
Fw 190 Single-Seat Pursuit Fighter
Bremen, 27 July 1938

Title page from Technical Description
No. 187.
Author's note: This technical description originates from 27 July 1938. In
our opinion, this is the earliest edition
of this technical description. If one
studies the text carefully, it becomes
apparent that a number of changes
were made to the Fw 190 prior to its
first flight. For example, the technical
description includes an electrically-
actuated main undercarriage, when in
fact the V1's undercarriage was hy-
draulically-actuated.

A. General

In addition to good handling characteristics and performance, the following conditions had to be met in the design of this single-seat pursuit fighter:

Shortest possible manufacturing time,
achieved though simple design, extensive breakdown and avoidance of excessive fitting work;
maximum operating reliability through the avoidance of complicated systems, which experience has shown to be a source of problems, liquid cooling, hydraulics, etc.,
ease of serviceability through good accessibility and organized arrangement of parts to be serviced;
protection for the pilot in the main directions of fire by the engine and fuel tank.

These requirements led to the design of a cantilever low-wing monoplane with a retractable undercarriage and powered by an air-cooled radial engine. Despite the engine's relatively large diameter, through careful aerodynamic shaping and restricting dimensions it was possible to achieve good handling characteristics. Emphasis was placed on good turning ability and the use of simple aids to reduce landing speed.

To reduce construction time and allow the aircraft to be built by unskilled labor, the entire structure was kept as simple as possible. The fuselage, wing and tail section are of Dural monocoque construction and are divided in such a way that they can be manufactured as shells. An engine mount was dispensed with and the engine is attached directly to the fuselage. The wing is separate from the fuselage and is attached to the fuselage by flanges. This makes it possible to dispense with expensive fittings and fitting work.

Split flaps have been selected to reduce landing speed, as much higher demands on the precision of shop work must be made with all other landing aids. The design of the retractable undercarriage was also kept as simple as possible. The two mainwheel legs and the tailwheel legs are retracted into the wing and fuselage by means of cables and electrically-driven cable drums[1]. The undercarriage lowers under its own weight.

The choice of an air-cooled engine was influenced by the requirement for a system which is reliable and easy to maintain. The absence of liquid cooling eliminates a common source of problems and significantly improved access to the engine. Moreover, the weight of the engine, and thus gross weight, is less than that of a liquid-cooled engine of the same power.

The placement of a protected fuel tank directly behind the pilot protects him from fire from the rear. The cockpit canopy provides a good view to the rear and is designed to allow the pilot to escape should the aircraft overturn.

Arrangement of the instruments where they may easily be seen and simple controls reduce pilot workload, allowing him to concentrate on flying and fighting. All components which require frequent monitoring or servicing are easily accessible, either directly or by means of large access panels. In addition to flight and engine instruments, the equipment includes the radio and oxygen systems. Planned armament consists of two MG 17s with 1,000 rounds of ammunition and two MG 151s with 320 rounds. Fuel capacity is sufficient for 1.5 hours of flight at 80%

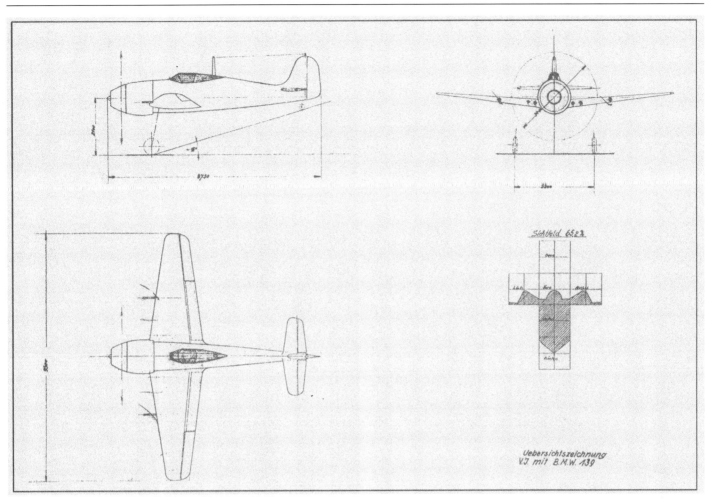

General arrangement drawing of the single-seat pursuit fighter.

power. Gross weight is 2750 kg with the BMW 139 engine installed. It must be borne in mind that the entire airframe (fuselage, undercarriage, tail section, controls and wing) weighs just 616 kg. The weight distribution, equipment and flight performance are described herein.

B. Technical Description

1.) Fuselage

The fuselage is a Dural monocoque structure. The forward part is almost circular and tapers into the tail section. In the interests of cheap and simple production, the fuselage is divided into three open shells by three join lines which are almost parallel to the direction of flight. These shells are manufactured separately and then riveted together. All rivet sites are easily accessible. Directly in front of the tail section a partition line square to the direction of flight divides the fuselage into two parts, which are bolted together and thus easily separated.

The center and rear spar attachment frames absorb the flexing forces from the wing, and the torsion is fed directly into the fuselage side wall by a flange connection. The floor and the bulkhead beneath the oil tank are designed as load-bearing elements. Their purpose is to transmit the engine forces into the fuselage side walls. There is no engine mount, and the engine is attached directly to the most forward fuselage frame.

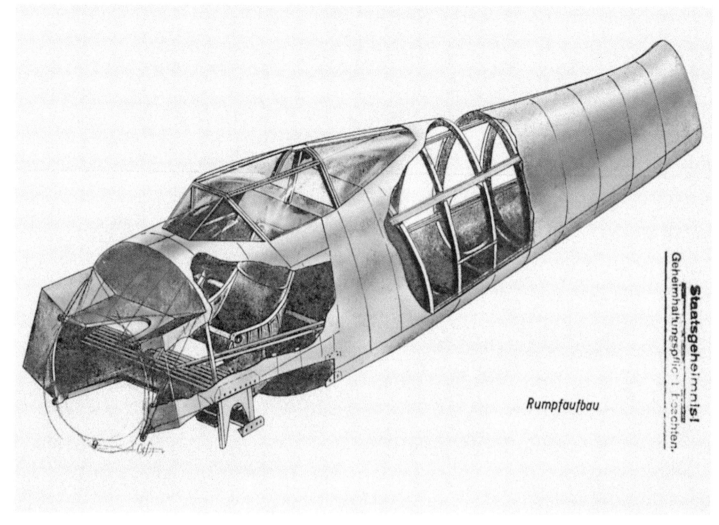

Rumpfaufbau

Staatsgeheimnis!
Geheimhaltungspflicht beachten.

Perspective view from the technical description.

The cockpit is covered by an a streamlined fairing. The canopy center section may be slid backward and can be locked in any position. To facilitate entry to and exit from the cockpit, flaps have been placed in the fuselage sides. These also enable the pilot to escape should the aircraft overturn. The sliding portion of the canopy can be jettisoned in an emergency.

The flat main vision panels are made of Siglas. The fixed rear portion of the canopy is made of Plexiglas, providing a good view to the rear as well. A rotating seat back enables the pilot to turn his upper body without loosening the shoulder harness.

The pilot's seat has a vertical adjustment range of 100 mm. It is mounted on the fuselage underside cross-bearing and is braced against the bulkhead at the rear of the cockpit. Large removable panels and hand holes plus a large access panel in the fuselage provide access to the controls and accessories. A retractable ladder in the fuselage is planned to ease entry to the cockpit. Located behind the cockpit is the fuel tank compartment, which is accessible through a removable panel on the underside of the fuselage.

2.) Undercarriage

The undercarriage consists of two main legs mounted in the wing, which retract into openings in the wing and fuselage square to the direction of flight. The two brake wheels have dimensions of 650 x 180 mm. When retracted, they lie in the fuselage directly behind the engine. Shock absorption is provided by VDM air shock struts, the upper end of which forms a circular mounting piece. Mounted on the bottom end of the strut is an axle flange with the cantilever wheel axle. The shock struts are braced by folding struts at right angles to the direction of flight. Torque links between the cylinders and pistons of the shock struts ensure that the wheels track properly.

The undercarriage is retracted by means of a cable which is attached at the bottom attachment points of the folding struts and led by pulleys to an electrically-driven cable drum. In the retracted position the undercarriage is held in place by a pawl. The undercarriage openings are covered by two mainwheel doors on the fuselage and two fairings attached to the shock struts and wheels.

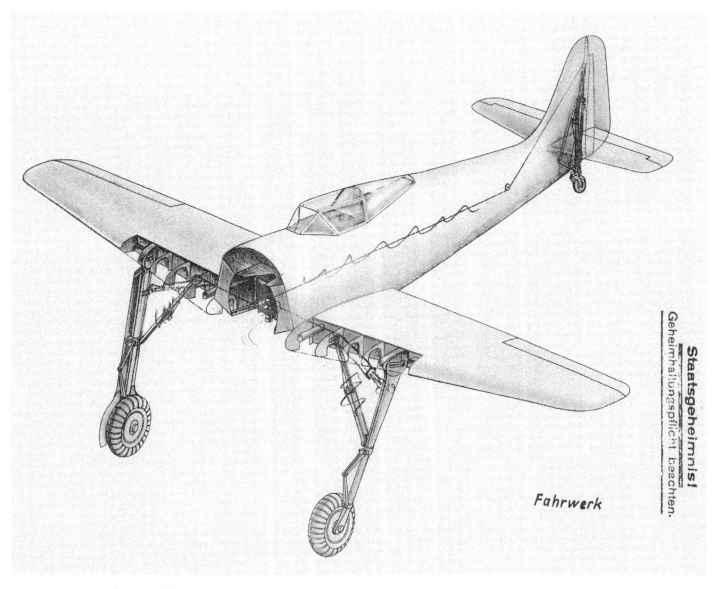

Staatsgeheimnis!
Geheimhaltungspflicht beachten.

Fahrwerk

The undercarriage of the Fw 190 V1 underwent several changes prior to its first flight.

The two main undercarriage legs are lowered by their own weight. A spring in the hinge of the folding strut pushes the struts slightly beyond the dead center position, making it impossible for the undercarriage to fold inwards during taxiing. The large wheelbase of 3.20 meters combined with wheel brakes ensure good taxiing characteristics.

The tailwheel has a pivoting 200x100 mm solid rubber tire and is equipped with an air shock strut. The tailwheel leg is attached to the vertical stabilizer spar, directly at the top and by guide a at the bottom. The head of the strut can be moved upwards by a cable in a straight line motion, retracting the tailwheel into the rear fuselage as far as the axle. The portion of the tailwheel outside the fuselage can serve as an emergency tailskid. Lowering of the tailwheel is achieved by its own weight, assisted by a spring which is tensioned when the tailwheel is retracted. The tailwheel is capable of rotating 360 degrees. On takeoff a return mechanism places the tailwheel in the center position.

To avoid confusion with other controls, the common operating lever for both main undercarriage legs and the tailwheel is placed within easy view of the pilot. Indicator lamps on the instrument panel show the positions of the main undercarriage and tailwheel.

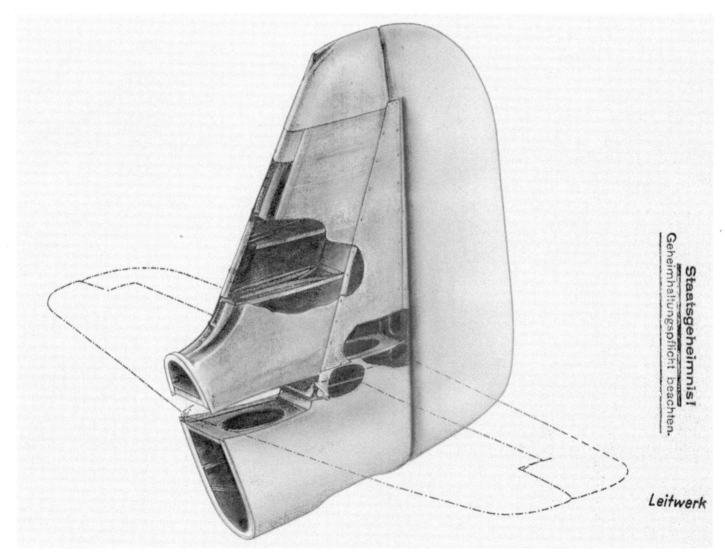

The characteristic outline of the Fw 190's tail section is visible in this initial layout.

3.) Tail Section

The cantilever horizontal stabilizer is a light metal design with a spar and a metal leading edge in the form of a torsion tube. For production reasons the stabilizer is split chordwise, allowing it to be manufactured in two open shells. It is attached to the vertical stabilizer spar in two places. The third mounting point on the leading edge is adjustable, allowing trim changes to be made in flight.

The elevator is in two parts. Both parts are interchangeable and are attached by means of a coupling. Each consists of a torsionally-stiff metal leading edge with ribs riveted to it and is fabric-covered. The elevators are completely weight balanced and have a horn balance. The vertical stabilizer is integral with the removable rear fuselage and is split chordwise like the horizontal stabilizer. Its structure is similar to that of the horizontal stabilizer.

The structure of the vertical stabilizer is similar to that of the horizontal stabilizer. It is fabric-covered and has a torsion leading edge, to which ribs are riveted. In addition to a horn balance, which also acts as a weight balance, a trim tab is planned which is coupled with the throttle control rod. The ailerons also have a torsionally-stiff leading edge with riveted ribs and fabric covering. A manually-adjustable trim tab is intended to partly compensate for engine torque. The landing aids, in the form of split flaps, consist of a box spar with attached ribs and metal skinning on the underside. The split flaps extend across the inner part of the wing, covering approximately 60% of the wingspan. All control surfaces and the split flaps are mounted in three places in ball bearings.

4.) Flight Controls

The elevators and ailerons are operated by a conventional joystick. The hydraulic pumps for the wheel brakes are attached to the rudder pedals. Transmission of con-

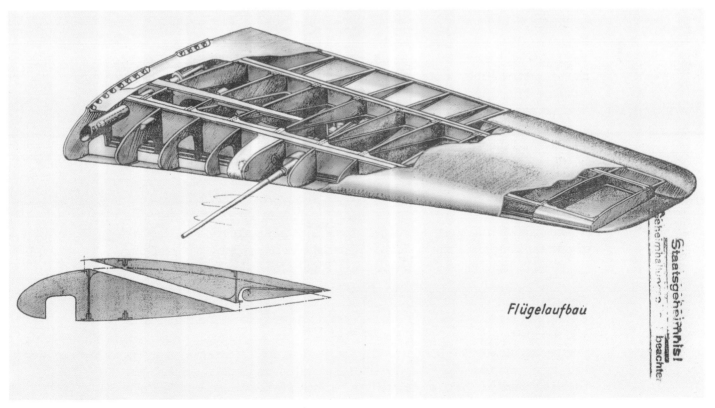

Flügelaufbau

Schematic drawing of the wing with two wing-mounted weapons.

trol movements for the elevators and ailerons is by control rods in the cockpit and fuel tank compartment, and by control cables in the aft fuselage. As a safety measure against battle damage, the elevator control rods are twinned. Control rods only are planned for the ailerons. In the area of the fuel tank the control rods are sheathed to prevent them from jamming in the event of a tank rupture. Tailplane incidence is adjusted by means of an electric motor with intermediate gearing. The associated control switch is located on the joystick. The rudder trim tab switch is coupled with the throttle lever, however it is possible to adjust the tab independently. An electrically-driven control rod is planned for lowering the landing flaps. The two ailerons are deflected approximately 10 degrees when the flaps are lowered.

5.) Wing

The cantilever wing has a trapezoidal outline with rounded tips and is of all-metal monocoque construction. Incidence measured on the upper surface of the wing is 4 degrees.

The two wing halves are flange-mounted to the fuselage and bolted in place. They are divided in such a way that the upper and lower shells can be made separately. After completion, the two shells are joined by several easily accessible riveted seams.

The static unit is formed by two spars and the metal skinning, which is stiffened by ribs and stringers. Because of the position of the mainwheels when retracted, the forward spar cannot be continued through the fuselage. An auxiliary spar will therefore have to be planned, which, together with the rear spar, can transfer the torsion forces into the fuselage.

A common bearer attached to the forward spar is planned for mounting the undercarriage and the outer wing weapons. Large access panels facilitate the servicing of weapons and control elements inside the wing.

6.) Power Plant

Engine:

The following specification for the BMW 139 twin-row radial engine, which is planned for installation, was provided by the manufacturer:

Type BMW 139, fuel-injected motor
User group FW
Performance:

Increased short-term output	1 min	1,500 h.p. (takeoff power)
Short-term output	5 min	1,410 h.p. at 4500 m
Increased continuous output	30 min	1,270 h.p. at 4900 m
Continuous output		1,150 h.p. at 5400 m
Fuel consumption at continuous power		
at height of 5400 m		225 g/h.p.

Air cooled with cooling fan
Weight: engine without accessories, with cooling fan 800 kg

Propeller:

A fully-automatic three-blade VDM variable-pitch propeller with a diameter of 3.40 meters is used.

Engine Installation:

The engine is mounted on an intermediate ring with shock-absorbing mountings. To enable quick engine changes, the ring I attached to the fuselage by four ball connections. The engine accessory section projects through the attachment frame, which serves as a firewall, into the fuselage, with a bulkhead toward the cockpit. The wheels, which lie directly beneath the accessory section when retracted, are protected by an asbestos lining.

The air intake openings are located in the leading edge of the wing left and right of the fuselage. To avoid sharply bent intake shafts, the engine was turned about its longitudinal axis sufficiently to allow the intake openings to lie horizontally in the housing. According to information received from the manufacturer, a turn of about 13 degrees is safe.

Engine Cowling:

To minimize cowling drag at high speed, sharp curvatures, which lead to local speed spikes, had to be avoided in shaping the cowling. For this reason, the engine cowling was designed in such a way that it there is no step and only a slight curvature where it meets the propeller fairing. This, together with the fairing over the propeller hub, forms a ring-shaped nozzle through which cooling air is fed to the engine by means of a fan. The outflow of cooling air is regulated by split flaps on the underside of the fuselage. The engine cowling over the cylinders can be folded down, providing good access to all parts which require servicing. The forward part, into which the oil cooler is built, and the end of the cowling with intake shaft are permanently attached to the engine.

Exhaust System:

Ejector nozzles are planned to take advantage of the exhaust gas energy. The nozzles are distributed in such a way that the upper area with the cockpit fairing remains free. Deflectors on the fuselage sides prevent the main vision panels from becoming fouled and exhaust gas from entering the cockpit.

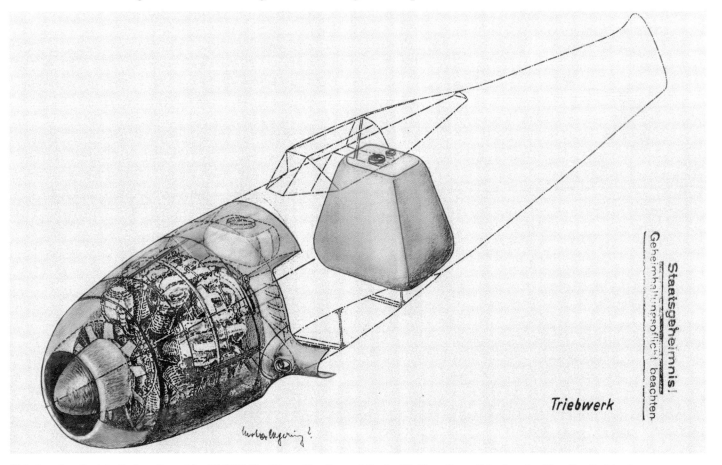

This drawing depicts the location of the BMW 139 with cooling fan and Focke-Wulf cowling, oil tank and self-sealing fuel tank.

Oil Tank:

The 16-liter oil tank, which is also provided with bullet-proofing, is located behind the engine above the engine accessories. To enable rapid engine changes, the tank is mounted on the engine cowling, allowing it to be removed with the engine.

C. Equipment

1.) Operating Systems

The *engine instruments* consist of an RPM indicator, twin pressure gauge for fuel and oil, boost pressure gauge, electric oil temperature gauge and electric fuel contents gauge with low fuel warning, and are arranged in front of the pilot in the instrument panel, which is mounted on vibration-absorbing mounts.

The *flight and navigation instruments* consist of an airspeed indicator and altimeter, plus fuel gauge, electric turn and bank indicator, back-up compass, clock and repeater compass from the Patin compass system, also in the instrument panel. The master compass is mounted in the rear fuselage and is easily accessible through a hatch in the fuselage side.

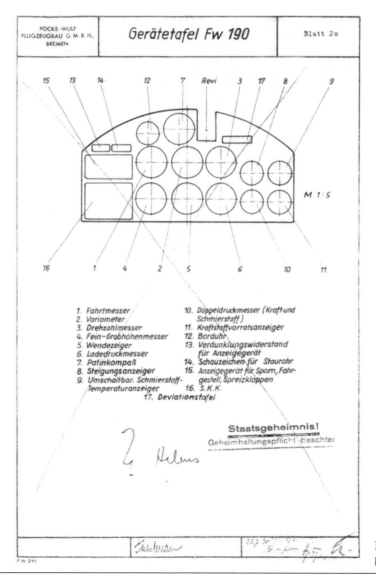

Instrument panel as originally planned for the Fw 190.

Identification Equipment: A flare pistol is located on the right next to the seat, within reach of the pilot. Signal ammunition for the pistol is housed in a box on the right cockpit wall.

Rescue and Safety Equipment: The pilot's seat is designed for a seat-type parachute and has adjustable shoulder and lap belts. Located on the right side of the cockpit is the high-altitude breathing system with valve and pressure gauge. A two-liter oxygen bottle is mounted on the fuselage frame behind the pilot's seat. The oxygen mask is located in a box next to the pilot's seat.

2.) Electrical Equipment

The engine drives a 1,000-Watt generator with an operating voltage of 24 Volts. It powers the electrical system through a regulator or charges the 7.5 ampere-hour accumulator. The various items of equipment are protected by circuit breakers. In the event of excess current, a magnetic remote-controlled master switch shuts off the entire electrical system.

The brightness of the instrument panel lights can be adjusted by means of a dimmer switch. The engine starting system consists of a Bosch A1/SQC 24 L 2 inertia starter, with electric and manual modes. Ignition current is provided through an external connection.

Undercarriage position can be monitored by an indicator device on the instrument panel. A Bosch horn, which sounds when the engine is at idle with the undercarriage raised, can be switched off by means of a push button when the pilot does not intend to land.

3.) Radio System

The aircraft is equipped with a FuG VII radio set, which is housed in the fuselage behind the pilot's seat between the center and rear spar attachment frames.

It is possible, however, to install other radio equipment with remote control. It is planned to run an antenna lengthwise to the vertical stabilizer.

4.) Armament

Armament consists of two MG 17s with 1,600 rounds and two MG 151s with 520 rounds of ammunition. The MG 17s have an electro-pneumatic cocking and firing system and are synchronized to fire through the propeller disc. They are located in the wing roots next to the fuselage and are easily accessible through large hatches on the upper surface of the wing. The ammunition boxes are located in the fuselage beneath the pilot's seat. The shell casings and links of the disintegrating belts are ejected.

The two MG 151s, which are cocked and fired electrically, are located in the wings outside the propeller disc. The ammunition boxes for the two weapons are located behind the boxes for the MG 17s. The belts are fed to the weapons by way of a channel in the wing.

Shell casings and empty belt links are ejected. These weapons are accessible through large hatches on the upper side of the wing.

The arrangement of the ammunition boxes in the fuselage and their ease of access means that the aircraft can be rearmed very quickly, thereby increasing its operational potential.

The planned aiming device is the C 12 c reflector gun sight.

Further details concerning the type and extent of the equipment and their locations can be found in the accompanying equipment list.

As this drawing of the weapons installation shows, the designers were still uncertain as to the distribution and location of the aircraft's armament when the technical description was issued. The Fw 190 underwent a number of changes even during the planning stage.

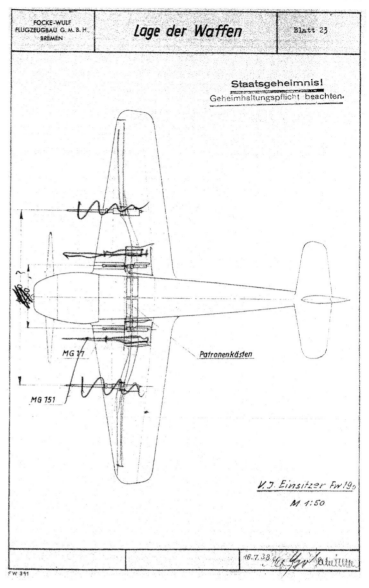

Table of Weights for the Fw 190				
Purpose: Single-Seat Pursuit Fighter				
1 Airframe	626 kg			
2 Power plant	1180 kg	Empty weight	1894 kg	
3 Total equipment	88 kg			Equipped weight 2107 kg
4 Additional equipment	213 kg			Gross weight 2748 kg
5 Fuel and oil	430 kg	Total load	854 kg	
6 Crew	100 kg			Useful load 641 kg
7 Usable load	111 kg			

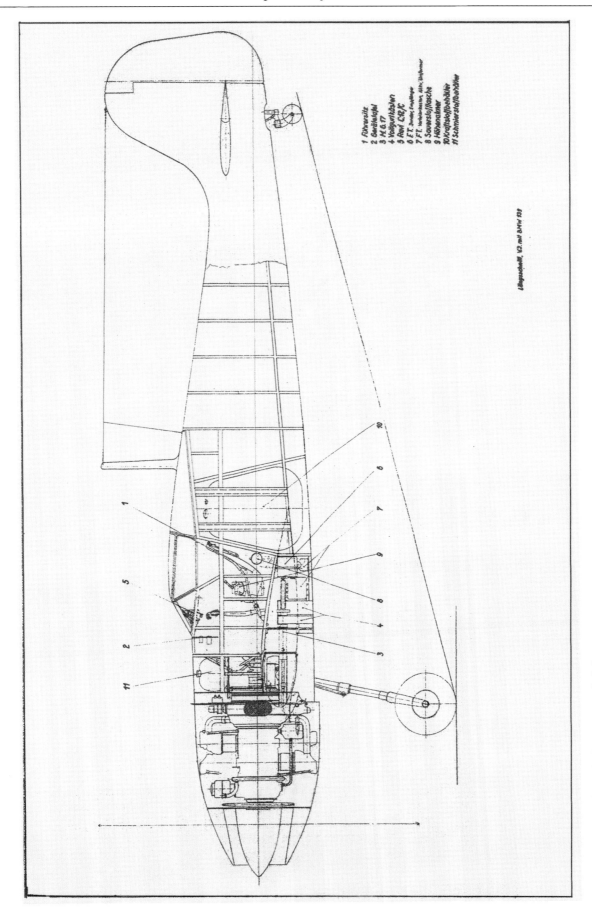

1 Führersitz
2 Gerätebrett
3 M.G.17
4 Vorderkühler
5 Revi C/12/C
6 F.T. Sender, Empfänger
7 F.T. Verkleidung, Abw. Störhörner
8 Sauerstoffflasche
9 Höhenatmer
10 Kraftstoffbehälter
11 Schmierstoffbehälter

Längsschnitt, V2, mit BMW 139

Cutaway drawing of the single-seat pursuit fighter.

Technical Description No. 187
Type Sheet No. 176-1

Type	Fw 190
Wing area	14.9 m²
Wingspan	9.50 m
Maximum height	3.40 m
Maximum length	8.65 m

Power plant	BMW 139
Engine output	1,460 h.p. at 2,400 rpm at 5600 meters
Propeller revolutions	1,290 rpm
Propeller	3-blade metal variable-pitch propeller, diameter 3.4 m

Performance at a Gross Weight of 2750 kg

Maximum speed at	height of	0 m	550 km/h
		2000 m	605 km/h
		4000 m	662 km/h
		5600 m	690 km/h
		7000 m	680 km/h

Maximum speed in level flight at 80% continuous power			
	At height of	0 m	500 km/h
		2000 m	555 km/h
		5000 m	640 km/h
		6500 m	670 km/h

Rate of climb at ground level		21 m/sec

Time to climb to	2000 m	1.6 min.
	4000 m	3.1 min.
	6000 m	4.9 min.
	8000 m	7.5 min.

Service ceiling		11 000 m
Landing speed		135 km/h
Endurance at 80% power		1.5 hr.
Range at	6500 m	1000 km

These performance figures were calculated taking into consideration the increase in maximum performance heights and engine power as a result of atmospheric pressure and the thrust effect gained by using ejector exhausts.

Many of the design features of the V1 are visible in this scale model.

paper from the rear edge of the engine cowling to the aircraft's tail. The fuselage, wing and tail were monocoque structures of Duralumin, which were manufactured as shells and then riveted together.

The two main undercarriage legs and the tailwheel were fully retractable, with an hydraulic retraction mechanism. The instruments and controls were laid out in such a way that the pilot could concentrate on flying the aircraft. Focke-Wulf was able to display the full scale mock-up of the Fw 190 to representatives of the RLM in 1938. Scale models were used to depict the layout of the external skinning for production of the prototypes.

Nothing was left to chance in the design of the Fw 190. The main problem in the development of the Fw 190 was time. In constructing the first Fw 190, Focke-Wulf made every effort to meet the deadline for the first flight. Rudi Blaser set up a field cot in the factory and slept there, so that he could be reached at any time to deal with a problem in the construction of the Fw 190. There were, of course, a few problems which had to be solved before the first flight. Rudi Blaser was extremely ambitious and was willing to do whatever it took to ensure that the Fw 190 was a success.

No one can better describe the initial development of the Fw 190 than the chief designer himself.

From Concept to Service Readiness

Memories of Designer Prof. Dipl.Ing. Kurt Tank

In the spring of 1938 the *Reischsluftfahrtministerium* (State Aviation Ministry) called upon the Focke-Wulf company to design a new fighter aircraft to supplement Messerschmitt's Bf 109, which was then just entering service.

My project department came up with a number of proposals, all of which anticipated a significantly more robust design than the Bf 109. One of these proposals was accepted and we received a contract to construct prototypes of the aircraft, which was designated the Fw 190. At the time we began work on the Fw 190, the Bf 109 and the British Spitfire were the fastest fighters in the world.

Both types were high-performance aircraft, which combined the most powerful engine available with the smallest possible airframe. Armament was a secondary consideration in the overall concept. These two types might be compared with race horses, which were capable of surpassing all competitors given good fodder and a smooth, flat track. When the track became more difficult, however, they tended to stumble.

Kurt Tank in conversation with Walter Nowotny during a visit by the highly-decorated airman to the Focke-Wulf factory.

From Concept to Service Readiness: Memories of Designer Prof. Dipl.Ing Kurt Tank

47

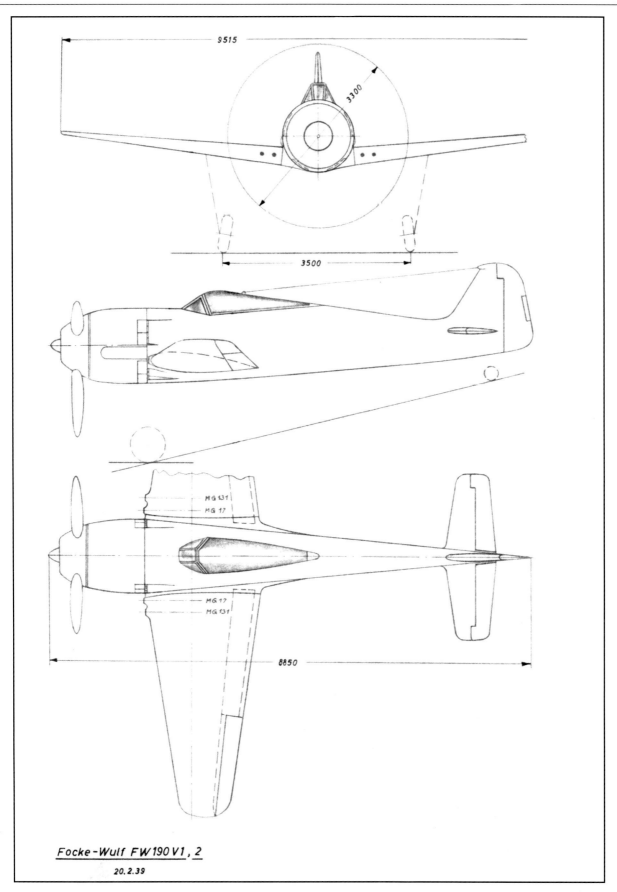

Focke-Wulf FW 190 V1, 2

20.2.39

This three-view drawing depicts the armament of the V1/V2, paired MG 17s and MG 131s in the wing roots. 20 Feb. 1939.

The BMW 139 devcloped 1,500 h.p. for take-off.

I had served with the cåvalry and the infantry in the First World War and there I saw the difficult conditions under which weapons and equipment had to remain operational and effective. I became convinced that in a future conflict another type of fighter aircraft, different from the Bf 109 and Spitfire, would have important roles to fill. It would have to operate from unprepared forward airfields, flown by mostly inexperienced pilots and serviced by hastily-trained personnel. These considerations influenced the design of the Fw 190, which was to be a "Service Horse", which is what the cavalry called their mounts, and not a racehorse. It was clear to me that a fighter of the earlier concept, designed primarily to be an interceptor, would be faster and climb better than my design with the same engine. It was our goal, therefore, to build a more robust machine which could carry a heavier armament, while ensuring that the difference in performance was not too great.

The basic concept of the Fw 190 was entirely conventional: at that time a low-wing monoplane with a single engine was the nest solution for a high-performance pursuit fighter. The low wing made it fairly simple to make the undercarriage retractable and did not seriously interfere with the pilot's field of view. From my own experience as a pilot,

I knew how important the best possible all-round view was for a fighter pilot, and we therefore designed a largely frameless hood for the new aircraft. In 1938, however, this was almost a new invention. We selected an air-cooled radial engine for two reasons. The first was that these engines were far more robust and reliable, even under difficult conditions. Secondly, the BMW 139 twin-row radial, which was under development by Bavarian Motor Works, produced 1,550 h.p., more than any contemporary liquid-cooled engine. We needed the most powerful engine available if our service horse was to approach the performance of the racehorses. Many people contend that my proposal for a fighter aircraft with a radial engine encountered resistance from the State Aviation Ministry. This may make for interesting history, but it is not the truth. In truth there was a significant group in the ministry which advocated such a fighter for the *Luftwaffe*. Testing of the Polikarpov I-16, examples of which had been captured in Spain, demonstrated the value of a robust fighter with a radial engine. We also saw that other nations, particularly the USA, were pushing ahead with the development of high-performance radial engines for fighter aircraft, and we felt that Germany should not fall behind in this area. For all these reasons we chose an air-cooled radial engine for the Fw 190.

Fw 190 V1, WNr. 0001, in the prototype shop in the Bremen-Neuenlanderfeld factory.

It was a decision I never had to regret. The Fw 190 would demonstrate the insensitivity of its power plant to enemy fire on numerous occasions, from the very start of its service career. Fighters returned from missions showing no visible signs of damage in spite of having had complete cylinders shot away. Even with a shot-up oil cooler, aircraft were able to return to base. An aircraft equipped with a liquid-cooled engine that suffered similar damage would have been able to remain in the air for three minutes at best.

The design of the Fw 190, like all other aircraft, was a team effort. While it would have been possible for a single designer to design such an aircraft by himself, it would have taken perhaps eight years to complete the job, by which time no one would have had any interest in the aircraft, as it would have become obsolete. For a combat aircraft to be of interest, its design had to be completed quickly, therefore the cooperation of a design team was of vital importance.

My assistant Willi Kaether was responsible for coordinating the work. Rudi Blaser and his team designed the air-frame. He was an extremely intelligent, experienced engineer, who succeeded in meeting the strength requirements of individual airframe components while minimizing the use of materials and weight. Ludwig Mittelhuber led the group in the project department responsible for the Fw 190.

Hans Sander and Kurt Mehlhorn were to conduct initial flight trials, and very early on they were brought in on the design work as advisors, using their experience as pilots to assist in laying out the cockpit, arranging the instruments and designing the controls.

In all, twelve men were involved in designing the Fw 190. By 1938 it was already clear that the trend was towards ever heavier combat aircraft, and from the beginning the Fw 190 was designed with this development process in mind. The best example of this is the undercarriage of the Fw 190, which from the very first prototype was designed for a sink rate of 4.5 m/sec compared to the then standard value of 2.5 m/sec. This was done to deal with the expected increases in weight and speed over the development life of the aircraft.

Fw 190 V1, with the main undercarriage retracted.

This foresight paid off. The Fw 190's gross weight more than doubled during the course of its development, however the aircraft's undercarriage underwent only minor changes. I selected the undercarriage only as an example, for the strength of many other airframe components was much higher than required from the start, which proved extremely valuable as development of the aircraft progressed.

It was not enough just to come with a suitable design for the new aircraft, it also had to be good to fly. The secret of good handling characteristics was the design of the control surfaces and the tail surfaces. The control surfaces had to be sufficiently large and had to be balanced with great care, both statically and dynamically, for an under balance would have resulted in excessive control forces and insufficient control effectiveness. In designing the Fw 190, therefore, we devoted much effort to optimizing control surface forces and effectiveness. We elected to use control rods instead of the control cables used previously as they ensured play-free control activation.

By the spring of 1938 the Fw 190 V1, the first prototype, was ready to fly and we were able to test its flight character-

istics. Hans Sander made the initial flights, after which I flew it, and we found that its flight characteristics were good, as we expected. The extensive work on the controls and control surfaces had paid off. I always believed that the force exerted by the pilot should be minimal in all flight conditions, and that if the controls and control surfaces were properly designed it should be possible to carry out most maneuvers with two fingers on the stick.

Rate of roll is extremely important in aerial combat as it enables the pilot to change direction quickly. To minimize physical effort by the pilot and prevent premature fatigue, aileron control stick forces must not exceed 4 kp. After various experiments we reached the point where we wanted to be. When the stick was moved, the resulting aileron deflection was immediate and precise, with no tendency to yaw.

Compared to the ailerons, the rudder and elevators presented no problems. The elevator forces were not as critical, and the rudder forces at the pedals could be much higher, as the pilot was capable of exerting greater force with his feet.

After we had checked and set the control surface forces and completed balancing the control surfaces, we set about

The Fw 190 V1.

testing the aircraft's stability in the entire speed range. This was especially important, as a fighter pilot cannot always make the corresponding trim changes when the throttle is moved. For this reason the Fw 190 was not fitted with trim tabs which could be adjusted in flight. Instead it had fixed tabs on all control surfaces which served only to compensate for production tolerances during mass production of the aircraft. The horizontal stabilizer was movable, however, allowing the pilot to adjust the incidence and compensate for trim changes in flight.

The Fw 190 V1 flew satisfactorily, the only difficulties being caused by its power plant, as the rear row of cylinders of the BMW 139 tended to overheat. To reduce drag, the twin-row radial engine had been completely cowled. Cooling air entered through a central opening in the large propeller hub, was blown around the cylinders by a fan, and exited through a circular opening behind the engine with slightly increased pressure. Flight trials revealed that, while this cowling did reduce drag somewhat, the resulting increase in speed was

insufficient to justify the expected cooling difficulties. And so, early in the course of testing, a more conventional cowling was adopted, similar in shape to a NACA cowling.

Even before the Fw 190 V1 took off on its first flight, BMW of Munich had offered the new BMW 801, a development of the BMW 139, which was just completing its test runs. Apart from the increase in power of 50 h.p., later 200 h.p., the new engine was supposed to be more reliable and less prone to overheating than the BMW 139. Shortly after the Fw 190 V1's maiden flight, we received instructions to change the design of the aircraft to accept the new BMW 801 engine. The result of this redesign was the Fw 190 V5, which first flew some time in the spring of 1940. Although engine output had increased by 50 h.p., engine weight had climbed by 160 kg. Further increases resulted from necessary reinforcements of the airframe, the addition of armor and changes in equipment required by the *Luftwaffe*. All of this increased the aircraft's weight by about one quarter of the original weight of the V1. Wing loading rose from 187 kp/m^2 to 228 kp/m^2,

The BMW 139, which powered the V1 and V2, prior to installation.

and maneuverability was reduced considerably. We now set about to make design changes to restore the good flight characteristics demonstrated by the Fw 190 V1.

We increased wingspan by about one meter and also increased the chord, as a result of which the wing became less markedly trapezoidal in shape. With this increase in wing area of approximately 3.2 m² wing loading was reduced to 177 kp/m².

Later we also increased the size of the horizontal tail surfaces to restore the optimal relative sizes of the two surfaces. From then on, the wing and horizontal tail of all versions of the Fw 190 designed for operation at low and medium altitudes remained unchanged until production ended. In the beginning we also had cooling problems with the BMW 801. These were far less serious than those with the BMW 139, however, and soon they had been overcome to the extent that failures were kept within acceptable limits.

Far more serious were problems with the BMW 801's *Kommandogerät* (control device), which was supposed to eliminate the need for the pilot to manually control various engine functions, such as mixture regulation, ignition timing, boost pressure, supercharger stage selection and propeller pitch. All the pilot had to do was operate the throttle; everything else was taken care of by the *Kommandogerät*, although in the beginning this only happened in theory. In practice, unfortunately, things were very different. Nothing worked the way it was supposed to, and the most unpleasant was the automatic shift in gears by the supercharger on reaching an altitude of 2600 meters.

During a test flight in one of the first prototypes I was supposed to make a loop at medium altitude. At first everything went as desired and I pulled up into the loop. At the top of the loop, with the machine inverted and speed at its lowest, the *Kommandogerät* suddenly switched into high gear, as I had just reached 2600 meters.

At that low speed I had little control over the aircraft. The sudden change in propeller moment sent it off course and it entered a spin. I lost my orientation, as the artificial horizon was not working and low cloud prevented me from seeing the ground. I could not tell if I was in a normal or an

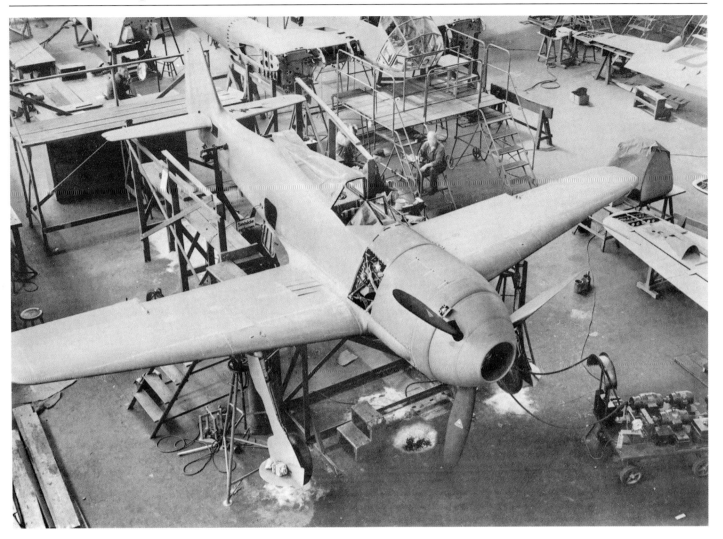

The Fw 190 V1 in near completed condition. Still missing are the propeller spinner in the Focke-Wulf double cowling, the panels behind the exhausts, and the panel over the tailplane incidence motor.

inverted spin. After various attempts and the loss of considerable altitude, I succeeded in getting out of the spin and was able to land safely. This incident gave me serious cause to think, however.

Immediately after landing I called the BMW company and informed them that I could equip the Fw 190 with another engine if they could not eliminate the problems with the engine and its awful *Kommandogerät*. The system was corrected and it later performed well in service, but we had to fight many battles before this was achieved.

When the Fw 190 entered service in the summer of 1941 it soon proved itself to be much superior to its opponents.

The enemy "Racehorses" treated our "Service Horse" with a great deal of respect. This situation lasted for almost a year and was not altered until the Spitfire Mark IX powered by a new Rolls Royce Merlin engine with a two speed supercharger entered service. With this new engine the Spitfire was superior to the Fw 190 at heights above 7500 meters. There is no doubt that the concept of the "Service Horse", which we selected for the Fw 190, was sound. Soon after the war I was invited to attend the airshow o the Society of British Aircraft Constructors at Hatfield. There was a large number of people in the Rolls Royce pavilion, including the famous British fighter pilot Johnny Johnson, whom I met.

When we were introduced he commented, "Oh, so you are the man who was responsible for the German fighter which caused us so many problems in 1942...."

Main undercarriage leg of the Fw 190 V1.

The First Fw 190 Takes to the Air

By the summer of 1939 the first prototype of the new Fw 190 was ready to fly. At the Bremen factory preparations for the first flight proceeded at a high tempo. Had the enormous efforts by Focke-Wulf in development, design and prototype construction paid off? During initial taxiing trials, test pilot Hans Sander, who was to make the first flight, methodically familiarized himself with the new machine.

On 1 June 1939 all was ready. Focke-Wulf personnel pushed the Fw 190 V1, D-OPZE, out of the hangar in Bremen.

Hans Sander started the BMW radial engine and taxied slowly to the runway. He advanced the throttle and after a run of about 300 meters the V1 lifted from the ground.

From the very beginning, Hans Sander was enthusiastic about the machine. The Fw 190 behaved magnificently in the air. Powered by the 1,550 h.p. BMW 139 radial engine, the aircraft accelerated quickly and on its very first flight demonstrated its excellent rate of climb. Sander flew the V1 twice on that day. The design appeared to be a success.

Fitter Willi Eckstein checks out the V1. The aircraft has no markings and has yet to be flown.

Hans Sander runs up the engine of the Fw 190 V1.

During company flight trials the V1 wore the civilian registration D-OPZE.

Chief designer Rudolf Blaser felt a great weight lifted from his shoulders. He identified himself very strongly with the design, but now his exhaustion became noticeable and he had to be sent away to rest and recuperate. All was not well with the new aircraft, however. Hans Sander very soon came to feel the almost unbearable heat in the cockpit, especially in the area of the feet. No provision had been made for cockpit ventilation. Inadequately sealed joints allowed exhaust gases to enter the cockpit, forcing the pilot to wear his oxygen mask. Problems were also encountered with retraction of the undercarriage. After a handful of flights, and the elimination of the undercarriage problem, the V1 was ordered flown to the test station at Rechlin.

On 3 July 1939 a so-called "Führer Demonstration" took place at Rechlin, where the latest aircraft developments were shown to Hitler, Göring, Udet and other senior officials. By order of the supreme command of the *Luftwaffe*, the fastest German fighter aircraft and most modern bombers were put on display and in some cases flown. Among the types on display were aircraft still in the prototype phase, such as the Fw 190, which could not be expected to enter service in the near future. Two months later the Second World War began.

The Fw 190 V1 was one of the aircraft flown for Hitler. After the demonstration the prototype was flown back to Bremen. In July the V1 logged a total of twelve hours in the air with no significant difficulties. A number of structural

The double cowling of the Fw 190 V1. Clearly visible is the main undercarriage hydraulic cylinder.

The unarmed V1 impressed Hans Sander from the very first flight.

Generalingenieur Lucht and Generaloberst Ernst Udet in conversation with Dipl.-Ing. Francke, easily identifiable in the light-colored clothing which he wore on account of the high temperatures in the cockpit of the V1.

The prototype received an excellent assessment at Rechlin. The only negative was the performance of the unreliable BMW 139.

For the Rechlin demonstration, D-OPZE was finished in standard three-tone camouflage.

Facing page, top:
The V1 on final approach.

Facing page, bottom:
The V1 on the runway.

Left: In-flight photo of D-OPZE.

changes were supposed to help solve the Fw 190's problems. The double cowling, which had been developed by Focke-Wulf and which gave the Fw 190 V1 its distinctive appearance, did not prove as successful as hoped, providing insufficient cooling of the BMW 139 radial. In the winter months that followed, therefore, the V1 was modified, with an NACA cowling replacing the Focke-Wulf double cowling. In the intervening period the Fw 190 V2 was also completed. Bearing the manufacturer's code RM+CB, the V2 completed its maiden flight on 30 November 1939. The engine cooling of the V2 did not function much better than that of the V1. The rear bank of cylinders overheated while the engine was being warmed up. In an effort to solve the problem once and for all, BMW delivered a cooling fan with adjustable blades for tests, however this did not produce any significant improvement.

Work was halted on the Fw 190 V3 and V4. Development of the BMW 139 was officially halted by the RLM. With the approval of the RLM, BMW turned to a new development, the BMW 801. Not only did the new engine offer improved cooling, it also produced nearly 200 h.p. more than the BMW 139. The airframe of the Fw 190 now had to be adapted to accommodate the new BMW 801. While the V3 was later used as a source of spare parts for the V1 and V2, the V4 was built as a structural test airframe for the first two prototypes.

The Minister of Air Armaments Ernst Udet and Generalingenieur Lucht examine the Fw 190 V1.

The Fw 190 V1, now wearing the manufacturer's code FO+LY. It first flew with the BMW 139 and NACA cowling on 25 January 1940.

Focke-Wulf billed the RLM 71,940 *Reichsmark* for the work that had already been done on the V3. In February 1940, during performance measuring flights with the V1, the cooling fan broke for the first time. Focke-Wulf wanted to dispense with the cooling fan entirely and began trials with the V2 without the fan. These had to be abandoned, however, as cooling proved inadequate when the aircraft was on the ground. No armament was installed in the V1 during flight testing, and the Fw 190 V2 was the first aircraft to carry weap-

ons. It was originally intended to install two MG 17 and two MG 131 machine-guns in the wing roots. On 2 March 1940, during weapons trials, the V2 overturned on landing and had to be returned to Bremen for repairs. Trials with the repaired V2 were resumed at Tarnewitz in September 1940. The V1 began flight trials at Rechlin at about the same time, arriving there on 11 June 1940. In the period from 28 June to 26 September 1940 Rechlin test pilot Heinrich Beauvais logged a total of six flights in the V1, which by then had a new

FO+LY in RLM camouflage and with solid-rubber tailwheel.

The BMW 139 with cooling fan and annular oil cooler was only an interim solution for the Fw 190.

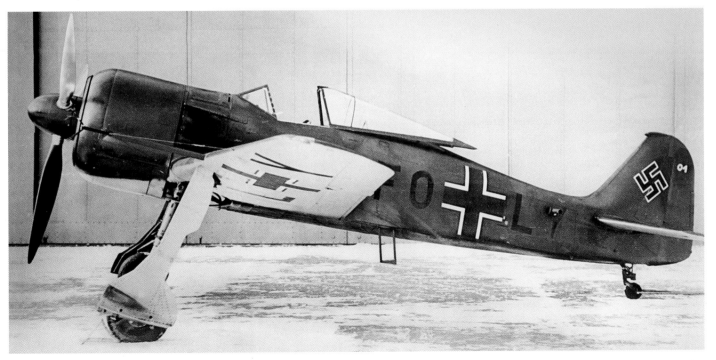

Flight trials with the troublesome BMW 139 engine took place in the winter of 1939-40. By that time approval had already been given for production of the BMW 801.

On 4 March 1940 the V2 overturned at Tarnewitz during weapons trials. The aircraft was subsequently returned to Bremen for repairs.

The windscreen and canopy were crushed when the V2 overturned. The tail section, which was flange-mounted to the rest of the fuselage, was also heavily damaged in the accident.

FO+LY in the winter of 1940.

manufacturer's code, RM+CA. Focke-Wulf continued to fly the V1 and V2 until at least mid-1943. The two machines retained the BMW 139 engine during the entire time they were under test. After that their trails disappear. It appears that the cooling problems with the BMW 139 were at least held within acceptable limits throughout this long test period. Unlike all later variants of the Fw 190, the V1 and V2 had undercarriages which retracted hydraulically and solid rubber tailwheels. Five years later the Ta 152 high-altitude fighter returned to an hydraulic undercarriage system.

The Fw 190 V1, FO+LY, in flight.

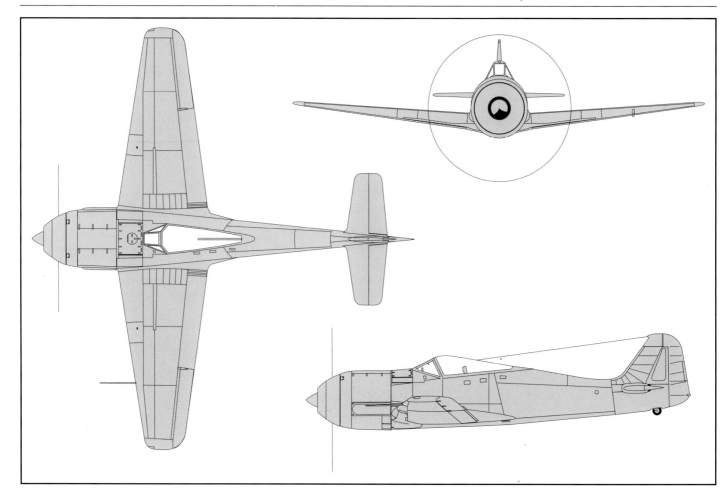

Fw 190 V1 Technical Data

Wingspan	9515 mm
Length	8850 mm
Propeller diameter	3300 mm
Wing area	14.9 m²
Undercarriage wheel track	3500 mm
Main undercarriage	650x180 mm, hydraulically-operated
Tailwheel	220x105 mm (solid rubber), hydraulically-operated
Gross weight	
V1	3020 kg
V2	3125 kg
Power plant	14-cylinder BMW 139 twin-row radial engine producing 1,550 h.p. for takeoff for one minute on the ground
Performance	
Maximum speed	690 km/h at 5600 meters
Rate of climb	21 m/sec at ground level
Range	max. 1000 km at cruise power (at 6500 m)
Service ceiling	11000 m
Takeoff distance	300 m
Landing speed	135 km/h

My First Flights in the First Fw 190s

Memories of Chief Test Pilot Hans Sander

I have flown many good aircraft in my time, but I cannot recall another aircraft which impressed me more from the very first flight than the magnificent Fw 190. From the first moment on, when I saw the small well-proportioned fighter in the final assembly hall, I had lost my heart. When I flew the first prototype for the first time on 1 June 1939, I was not disappointed in any respect.

This prototype was powered by a BMW 139 radial engine, the predecessor of the later BMW 801, which powered the third and all subsequent prototypes.

The engine was cooled by flaps, but the second row of cylinders tended to overheat a little, and when the flaps were closed the cockpit quickly overheated. During these test flights I always felt like a steak on a grill. These early difficulties were overcome, however, and everyone who flew the Fw 190 was enthusiastic.

In August 1940 I made a routine test flight in the third prototype, the Fw 190 V5k. It was several minutes after sundown, and I circled the field several times in preparation for landing. The few aircraft parked at the edge of the airfield

Hans Sander was associated with the Fw 190 throughout its entire development.

Wing armament mock-up for the Fw 190 V2.

were camouflaged with large nets, which were dragged around the airfield by a tracked vehicle. I saw the tractor while on approach, but I paid it little mind, assuming that the tractor driver had seen me and would therefore drive along the edge of the airfield. I lowered the undercarriage and throttled back the engine. The landing was perfect and I rolled along the runway at medium speed.

The big BMW 801 engine obscured the view forward, but the tractor driver, who had not seen me on approach to land, suddenly heard the sputtering engine sound of a landing Fw 190. He jumped from his seat and ran for his life.

In the next few seconds, with the sound of bending metal in my ears, I felt myself lifted up and then falling.

Then I lost consciousness. I must have been unconscious for several seconds. When I came to, I found myself hanging

The V2, RM+CB, still with the original Focke-Wulf canopy.

Fitters at work on the V1 in the Focke-Wulf prototype shop.

upside down in my straps. I became aware of the acrid smell of hot oil and feared that the machine was about to catch fire. I struggled like a madman in my efforts to free myself and, bleeding from countless wounds, I pounded on the shattered canopy. I succeeded in freeing myself. I staggered to a safe distance from the aircraft, but fortunately it did not burn.

I made countless test flights as the war went on. There was a constant stream of new variants of the Fw 190. Many of them underwent only minor changes for the testing phase. One was the planned Fw 190 high-altitude fighter equipped with a turbo-supercharger.

The aircraft was fitted with a Daimler Benz DB 603 engine with a large turbo-supercharger under the belly. These prototypes had no pressurized cockpit or deicing system for

the cockpit canopy. At high altitude a layer of ice formed over the entire canopy, blinding the pilot.

After a number of belly landings in the Fw 190, I found that the best means of safeguarding the fighter was to pay very close attention to one's surroundings during the flight back. Many service pilots who were obliged to force-land their Fw 190s survived belly landings with minor injuries. But for those who overturned on landing, it was a different story. I found out that the best thing to do when a belly landing became inevitable was to set the propeller pitch back as far as it would go. The propeller blades then acted like wheel chocks as soon as they touched the ground.

While we were testing aircraft, we Focke-Wulf test pilots also had to fly missions against Allied bombers attacking

our factories. We destroyed some, but we also lost some outstanding test pilots in this way.

Late in the war test flights between Bremen and Hamburg became impossible. We therefore moved to Hannover-Langenhagen in Lower Saxony, but the flying was not much better there, because we were on the bomber route to Berlin. The sky there was full of Allied bombers and their escort of Mustangs and Thunderbolts, which flew boisterously about them.

As the war went on, it became clear even to the greatest optimist that the war was lost. In spite of this obvious future, we continued out test flying until the end of the war.

Surprisingly, the Allies took us to Bad Eilsen, Focke-Wulf's last headquarters, but we knew this could not last long. My days of test flying were over.

WNr. 0001, RM+CA, with the BMW 139 and NACA cowling.

The Fw 190 and the BMW 801

The RLM halted development of the BMW 139 on 30 September 1939. Just one day later, the Bavarian Motor Works received the official development contract for the future BMW 801. From that day on, it was obvious that the Fw 190's only chance was with the new engine, as the BMW 139 had no future.

With the BMW 801 in the development stage, Focke-Wulf had no choice but to turn to the BMW 139. But the designers also knew that the BMW 801 would have to be worked into the Fw 190 airframe as soon as it was ready. Focke-Wulf received the first BMW 801 mockup in June 1939, roughly the time of the Fw 190 V1's maiden flight. At that time BMW was running the first three BMW 801 proto-

types on the test bench. By January 1940 BMW had all fifteen prototype engines on the test bench. At that time the V14 prototype engine was producing 1,800 h.p. and had completed a 100-hour run without complaints.

Building on the test results achieved with the Fw 190 V1 and V2, Focke-Wulf was able to begin construction of two more prototypes with the new BMW 801 engine. Focke-Wulf took advantage of the beginning factory trials of the BMW 801 to carry out a thorough redesign of the Fw 190. The most important innovation of the BMW 801, the single lever engine control with the so-called *Kommandogerät*, was not installed on the first engines. The *Kommandogerät* automatically controlled engine speed, boost pressure, the air-fuel

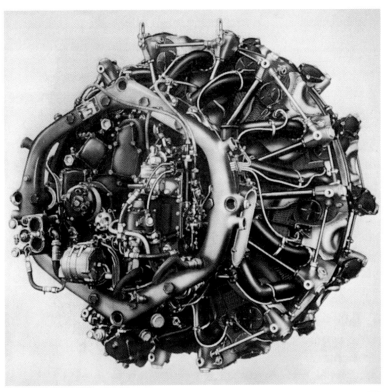

The 14-cylinder, twin-row BMW 801 C radial engine. Diameter: 1290 mm, volume: 41.8 liters, weight: 1055 kg. The specially-fitted mounting ring on the rear of the engine was attached to the airframe at four mounting points.

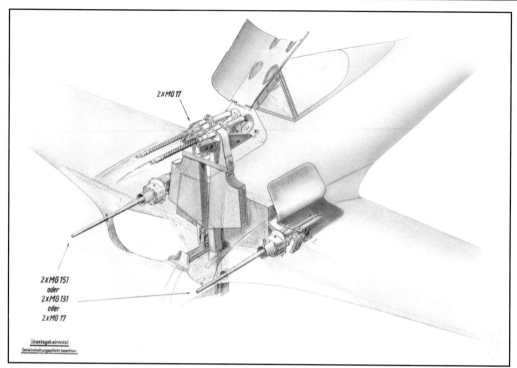

2x MG 17

2x MG 151
oder
2x MG 131
oder
2x MG 17

Staatsgeheimnis!
Geheimhaltungspflicht beachten.

Weapons installation of the V5 with small wing.

mixture, ignition timing and supercharger speed independent of altitude. This later significantly simplified engine operation by the pilot. The new engine also had a number of disadvantages, however. Not only was the BMW 801 160 kilograms heavier than the BMW 139, it was also 50 centimeters longer. The members of the design team responsible for the project, von Faehlmann and Mittelhuber, subsequently decided in favor of a fundamental modification of the forward fuselage.

The cockpit was moved farther back in the fuselage to compensate for the increase in weight. Moving the pilot's seat back would compensate for the rather longer BMW 801 and also significantly reduce the heat buildup in the cockpit to a bearable level. The installation of weapons in the fuselage of the V1 and V2 had been impossible for reasons of space. The room created between the firewall and instrument panel allowed the installation of a weapons system with ammunition. There had been similar problems with the wing of

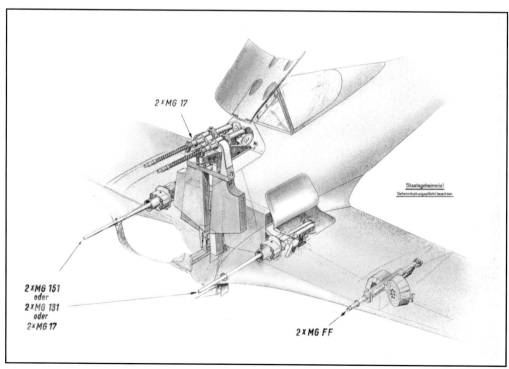

2 x MG 17

2 x MG 151
oder
2x MG 131
oder
2 x MG 17

Staatsgeheimnis!
Geheimhaltungspflicht beachten.

2 x MG FF

Weapons installation of the V5 with large wing.

From the left: the Fw 190 V5; the V2, RM+CA; WNr. 0 015, A-0/U11; and next to it an A-1 with the manufacturer's code KB+PJ.

WNr. 0 005 with the engine bearers, weapons installation, and windscreen frame.

The Fw 190 V5k with BMW 801 C.

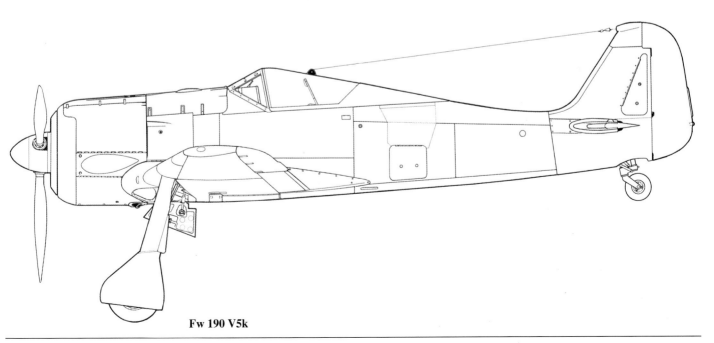

Fw 190 V5k

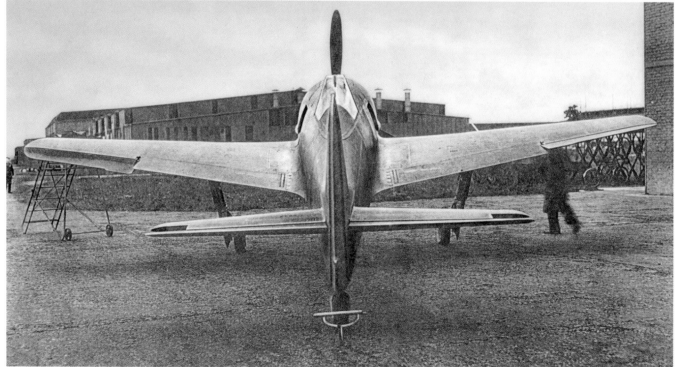

Fw 190 V5k: factory photo and data sheet.

Facing page: Factory photos of the V5k, still unpainted.

Type Sheet Fw 190 V5k

Type	Fw 190
Wing area	14.9 m²
Wingspan	9515 mm
Maximum height	3.72 m
Maximum length	8.95 m
Power plant	BMW 801 C-0
Takeoff power	1,622 h.p. at 2,686 rpm at ground level
Propeller	3-blade metal variable-pitch, D = 3.3 m

Performance at a gross Weight of 3200 kg

Maximum speed at takeoff and emergency power at		
	0 m	602 km/h
	5600 m	714 km/h
Rate of climb at ground level		17 m/sec
Time to climb to 6000 m		5.5 min.
Service ceiling		11000 m
Landing speed		144 km/h
Takeoff distance		300 m
Range		1100 km

Technical Data for the Fw 190 V5k

Wheel track	3500 m
Wheel diameter Main undercarriage Electrically operated	750 x 175 mm
Tailwheel Electrically operated	350 x 135 mm
Power plant: 14-cylinder BMW 801 C-0 twin-row radial engine	
Takeoff power:	1,600 h.p. for 3 min.
Engine volume:	41.8 l

The V5 was involved in a serious accident while being flown by Hans Sander and had to be scrapped.

the V1, which was split chord-wise. Focke-Wulf had difficulty fitting sufficiently large armament servicing hatches at the wing roots.

The problems with the weapons installation elicited the following question from Rechlin: "Do you want to set records with it or win the war?" One of those closely involved in reworking the Fw 190 into its ultimate form was Dipl.-Ingenieur Hans Helmsmüller. According to him[3], it was less von Faehlmann's efforts, rather the reworking of the design, that finally brought success to Focke-Wulf. Although the aircraft's external shape was largely retained, the design of the airframe and wing was completely changed.

A slight change in the mounting angle of the BMW 801 greatly simplified the installation of the two fuselage guns, allowing the machine-gun channels to be better integrated into the engine cowling. As a result of this the pilot's seat was lowered by 20 centimeters.

A minor reduction in visibility while taxiing was consciously accepted. The pilot's seat was reduced in size slightly and was equipped with armor plate to protect the pilot. The airframe was further improved through the optimal incorporation of the cockpit canopy into the fuselage lines. Technically, Helmsmüller created the conditions necessary for the installation of two MG FF cannon, two MG 131 machine-

guns or two MG 151 cannon in the outer wings. Using the experience he had gained working for Heinkel, in designing the Fw 190 he positioned the center of gravity in such a way that it scarcely moved when the ammunition and fuel tanks were emptied. A statement by Mittelhuber described how critical and tense the situation was in the design bureau: "If you stop, the bird (meaning the Fw 190) will be scrapped. If you fail, the bird will be cancelled. This is a Blaser design, every hour that is not spent working on the bird is wasted." The new prototypes would differ significantly from the first two prototypes, including structural changes. The wing roots were moved forward to create space for a heavy armament. The characteristic mainwheel fairings of the V1 and V2 were replaced by separate mainwheel and wheel well fairings. The tailwheel was increased in size, with an air-filled tire. Focke-Wulf also wanted to use the first of the new prototypes, the V5, to test two different wings. It was first flown with the old wing, which had an area of 12.6 m² and a span of 9.56 m. This was designated the "Small Wing". For comparison, the V5 would be fitted with a new wing with an area of 18.5 m² and a span of 10.50 meters, the so-called "Big Wing". Not until April 1940 did Focke-Wulf receive a BMW 801 C-0 engine (WNr. 80 110) for the Fw 190 V5. In an Engine Bench Run Report dated 15 March 1940 this BMW 801 produced

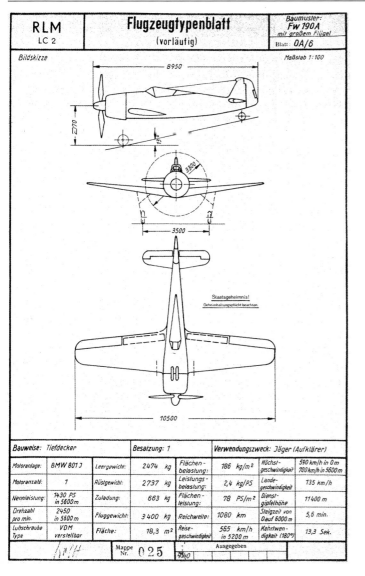

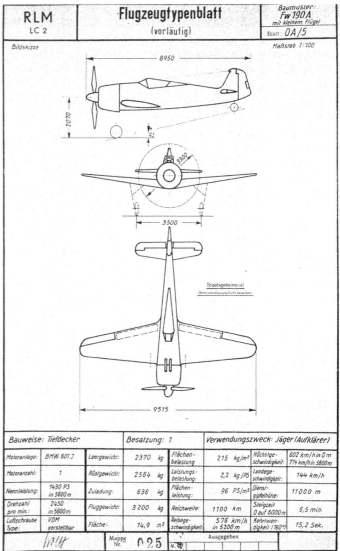

RLM LC 2	Flugzeugtypenblatt (vorläufig)	Baumuster: Fw 190A mit großem Flügel Blatt: 0A/6

Bildskizze — Maßstab 1:100

Staatsgeheimnis! Geheimhaltungspflicht beachten.

Bauweise: *Tiefdecker*		Besatzung: 1		Verwendungszweck: *Jäger (Aufklärer)*	
Motoranlage:	BMW 801 J	Leergewicht:	2474 kg	Flächen-belastung: 186 kg/m²	Höchst-geschwindigkeit: 590 km/h in 0 m 700 km/h in 5600 m
Motoranzahl:	1	Rüstgewicht:	2737 kg	Leistungs-belastung: 2,4 kg/PS	Lande-geschwindigkeit: 135 km/h
Nennleistung:	1430 PS in 5600 m	Zuladung:	663 kg	Flächen-leistung: 78 PS/m²	Dienst-gipfelhöhe: 11400 m
Drehzahl pro min.:	2450 in 5800 m	Fluggewicht:	3 400 kg	Reichweite: 1080 km	Steigzeit von 0 auf 6000 m: 5,6 min.
Luftschraube Type	VDM verstellbar	Fläche:	18,3 m²	Reise-geschwindigkeit: 565 km/h in 5200 m	Kehrtwen-digkeit (180°): 13,3 Sek.

Mappe Nr. 025 — Ausgegeben

RLM LC 2	Flugzeugtypenblatt (vorläufig)	Baumuster: Fw 190A mit kleinem Flügel Blatt: 0A/5

Bildskizze — Maßstab 1:100

Staatsgeheimnis! Geheimhaltungspflicht beachten.

Bauweise: *Tiefdecker*		Besatzung: 1		Verwendungszweck: *Jäger (Aufklärer)*	
Motoranlage:	BMW 801 J	Leergewicht:	2370 kg	Flächen-belastung: 215 kg/m²	Höchstge-schwindigkeit: 602 km/h in 0 m 714 km/h in 5800 m
Motoranzahl:	1	Rüstgewicht:	2584 kg	Leistungs-belastung: 2,2 kg/PS	Landege-schwindigkeit: 144 km/h
Nennleistung:	1430 PS in 5600 m	Zuladung:	636 kg	Flächen-leistung: 96 PS/m²	Dienst-gipfelhöhe: 11000 m
Drehzahl pro min.:	2450 in 5800 m	Fluggewicht:	3 200 kg	Reichweite: 1100 km	Steigzeit 0 auf 6000 m: 5,5 min.
Luftschraube Type:	VDM verstellbar	Fläche:	14,9 m²	Reisege-schwindigkeit: 576 km/h in 5200 m	Kehrtwen-digkeit (180°): 15,2 Sek.

Mappe Nr. 025 — Ausgegeben

Three-view drawings of the Fw 190 V5 with the small wing (left), and large wing (right).
Following page:
Company drawing of the large wing for the V5.

1,622 h.p. In the subsequent tests with the two wings, it turned out that the V5 was 10 km/h slower than the big wing, but was more maneuverable about all axes.

A decision was made in favor of the big wing. This wing would be retained by the Fw 190 until the end of the war. The second prototype, the Fw 190 V6, was fitted with the big wing from the beginning.

Both prototypes began type testing in the spring of 1940. In early 1941 the V6 was fitted with the small wing for the first time. On 9 September 1940 Hans Sander was involved in a serious accident in the V5, which had to be scrapped. This left only the V1, V2 and V6 for subsequent testing. By that time the performance of the V5 and V6 had proved so convincing that the RLM issued a contract for the construction of a pre-production series of 20, later 28 machines. For Focke-Wulf this RLM contract was the longed-for first success and convincing proof of the correctness of the direction it had taken in developing the Fw 190. The pre-production series was intended to allow Focke-Wulf to undertake broad-based testing of the Fw 190 in order to allow the single-seat fighter to enter service with the *Luftwaffe*.

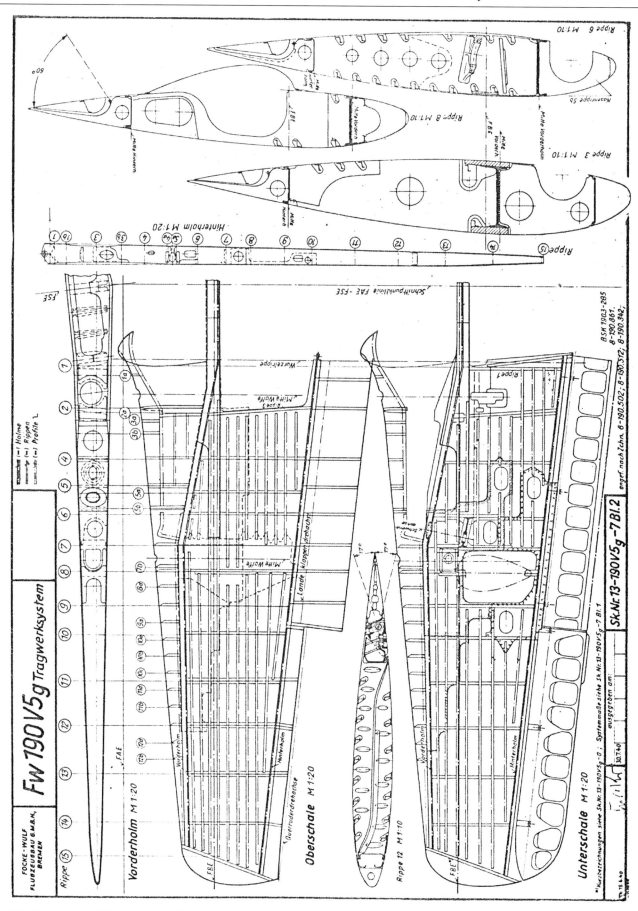

Focke-Wulf Fw 190 fighter with BMW 801 radial engine.

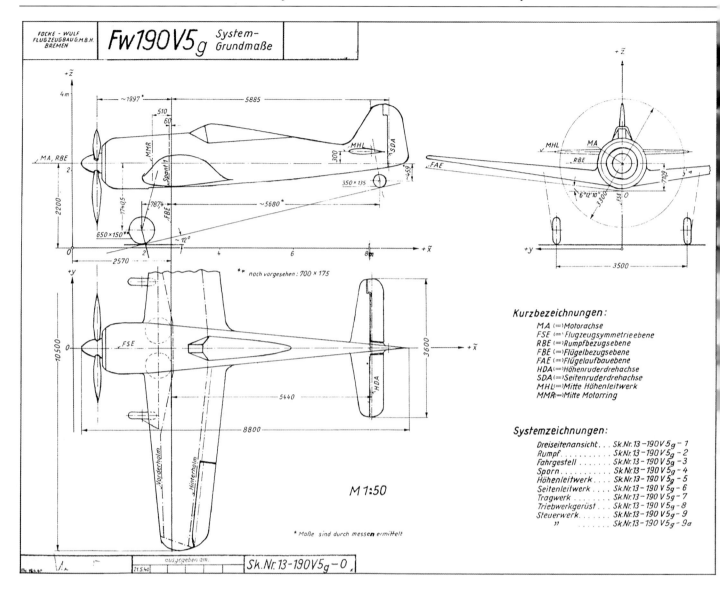

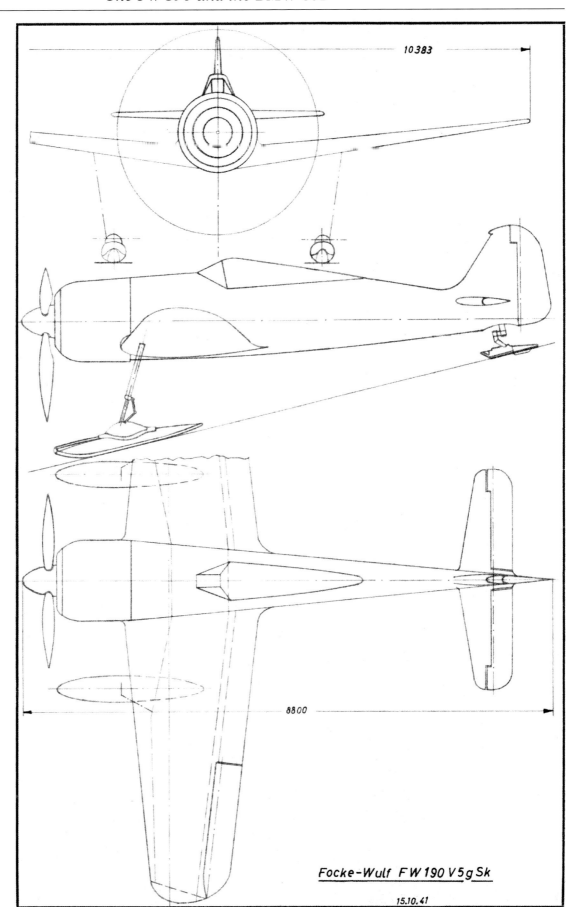

Focke-Wulf FW 190 V5g Sk

15.10.41

Facing page:
Factory drawing of the Fw
190 V5g dated 21 May
1940.

Facing page, bottom:
The redesigned wing was
tested in the wind tunnel.

Focke-Wulf projected a
ski-equipped version of the
Fw 190 based on the V5.

The 190 Against the 109

Heinrich Beauvais was one of the most successful and best-known test pilots of the former *Luftwaffe* test station in Rechlin. When the Fw 190 entered service with the *Luftwaffe*, the Messerschmitt Bf 109 had reached the peak of its performance.

For this reason, therefore, a comparison of the performance of the two aircraft from the point of view of a Rechlin test pilot carried special weight:

Heinrich Beauvais.

"Of interest was the comparison flight between the Bf 109 F-4 and the Fw 190 A-2 in the autumn of 1942. I made a number of flights with Gollob as my opponent, and as usual we took turns flying both aircraft.

Gollob's attitude was typified by his proposed radio callsigns: 'Adler' (Eagle) for him, and 'Otto' for me. It was alright with me—we would see!

First he flew the 109 and was at least superior in turning. This was a confirmation for Eagle and Otto, which he expressed with a superior chuckle when he outclimbed me.

The outcome of the next flight was the same as far as the types were concerned, but different with respect to Eagle and Otto. This at first seemed inexplicable in two respects. How could a civilian like me put on such a display?

We instinctively preferred the Fw 190 over the Bf 109 from the very start. The reasons for this were detailed in the report. The Fw 190's control forces were significantly lower at high speeds, and its rate of roll was markedly greater. Furthermore, its wide-track undercarriage and the superior rigidity of its airframe were highly thought of, especially for belly landings. The view to the rear was superior, and its BMW radial engine was less vulnerable to enemy fire. There was a tendency to disbelieve its inferiority in turning. The report stated that, 'It has yet to be determined whether the Fw 190 turns tighter than the Bf 109.' In my opinion this should be viewed as misleading. It is true that turning radii were not measured, but that did not really matter. What did matter was turning times, and in this respect the Bf 109 was clearly superior."

Heinrich Beauvais' experience with the Fw 190 extended back to the V1. He recalled:

"The Fw 190 V1's BMW 139 engine gave us uncomfortably hot feet. The Fw 190 needed barely four seconds to com-

Foreground: an A-0 with the small wing. In the background are WNr. 0019, KB+PU, designation Fw 190 A-0/U2, and an A-0/U13.

plete a complete roll, compared to five seconds for the Bf 109. The roll rate was particularly good with the original 15-square-meter wing.

We recommended to the Focke-Wulf people, 'Make the wing bigger!' The production aircraft was fitted with a wing of 18.3 square meters."

During his testing activities he also made a belly landing in a Fw 190:

"The BMW 801 engine's so-called *Kommandogerät* did not always work as it was supposed to. Once, after lowering the undercarriage, I found that advancing the throttle had no effect, making it impossible for me to reach the airfield. I retracted the undercarriage again and prepared for a belly landing in the area between Müritz and the barracks. At the last moment I saw a pedestrian in my landing direction. I had little altitude to work with, and so my evasive action took the

form of a crabbed landing. As a result the aircraft fishtailed on the ground, a 'Dutch Roll' as it were. This caused me to bang my head in the cramped cockpit, resulting in a head wound which bled quite heavily. After landing I was unable to open the canopy with the hand crank, and so I activated the canopy jettison system, which worked flawlessly. This aid had been installed because at 250 km/h the slipstream made it almost impossible to open the canopy by hand. In spite of the difficulties just described the landing was in fact quite harmless compared to Clostermann's 'dramatic description' of a similar incident in a Spitfire.

Finally Dr. Haller drove up and bandaged me on the spot. That evening there was a going away party for the familiarization unit. I attended with my bandaged head, 'like an old warrior' someone said. Franke subsequently sent me on leave, and I used the opportunity to go mountain climbing. Later 'Spez' Krammel of Focke-Wulf told me that I should have moved the throttle lever back and forth quickly, to release a stuck slide. Perhaps he was right."

Fw 190 A-0 pre-production aircraft.

In his writings Heinrich Beauvais also gives a very extensive description of the Fw 190's flight characteristics:

"Stall: even the Fw 190 lost lift at a certain angle of attack. A further influence was the bank angle. In practice this showed itself in straight flight, for example while landing. In general, however, the aircraft should only be a few centimeters above the ground when Camax is exceeded. An effort was made to enlarge the flaps to reduce landing run. As a result, a very precise pull-out became necessary to achieve a smooth landing and short roll-out. With excess speed everything became easier, only the distance required became greater, so that little was achieved for the 'normal case.' Of particular importance to a fighter pilot is the 'high speed stall.' During the comparison flights described earlier, Gollob at first refused to believe that an aircraft could be stalled in the 400 km/h speed range.

These trials also demonstrated that the Fw 190 did not turn as well as the Bf 109.

Loops: One day Schmitz said that it was difficult to loop the Fw 190, as it always turned away. He rejected the explanation that he had probably pulled back on the stick too hard. As we had a two-seater at our disposal at that time, we conducted an experiment.

When we had sufficient altitude, I said, 'Alright, you have it.' My colleague increased speed and then hauled back hard on the stick. With the aircraft semi-inverted, there was a slight jolt and the nose began to wander. No move was made to counter this, until I applied full rudder and thus maintained some sort of control over course and attitude. Then the bird dropped its nose slowly, straight down. I then proceeded to carry out a flawless loop without pulling back on the stick too hard. Schmitz's reaction: 'I see!'

BMW 801 C engine.

From left to right: V5k, WNr. 0005; V1, RM+CA, WNr. 0001; A-0/U11, WNr. 0015; A-0/U2, KB+PJ; and A-0/U4, WNr. 0022.

In the foreground is an A-0 with the short wing. Behind it is WNr. 0019, KB+PU, a Fw 190 A-0/U2.

Three-Point Takeoff: On 27 March 1943 Hans Sander delivered a 190 from Focke-Wulf to Rechlin. It was equipped with a TK 11 turbosupercharger and DB 603 engine. He wanted to get back to Bremen as soon as possible. I therefore rushed my takeoff and allowed the machine to lift off in a three point attitude. We had adopted this procedure from the front-line units, though not wholeheartedly and not without reservations. In this case it almost went wrong, for at a height of just a few meters the right wing suddenly dropped and the application of opposite aileron failed to correct the situation. For an instant I was at a loss. Then it came to me: 'Stall!' I had little time to think about it, however, and so I abruptly applied full left rudder and gave the stick a short push forward. This caused the aircraft's mainwheels to touch down, after which I was able to take off normally. No one had noticed.

Blinded: While on a night approach, just before touchdown, I was suddenly illuminated by an anti-aircraft searchlight. In this situation my only choice was to carry out an overshoot on instruments, which was also an extremely questionable

maneuver. I was taken completely by surprise, for no one had informed me about planned flights by a He 177 in a searchlight beam, and it is unlikely that anyone said anything about the Fw 190 to the searchlight people, who were commanded by Mannje Haagen. I had not seen the He 177, as it had taken off from Lärz. Obviously the whole thing had been poorly prepared. Either there was no radio contact between the He 177 and the flak or it wasn't working properly. It therefore was not extremely clever to look for the He 177 on the runway at Rechlin.

The next day Major Haagen apologized, which was admirable, although under the circumstances it probably didn't make much difference.

Takeoff Tests: Condensation trails were often seen at the wingtips or propeller tips. It was something new for us that an entire wing could become white in a dive. It was thought that wooden drop tanks would be unable to stand up to speeds achieved in a dive, and so I was to attempt to cause one to come apart. As I recall, at about 650 km/h there was a tre-

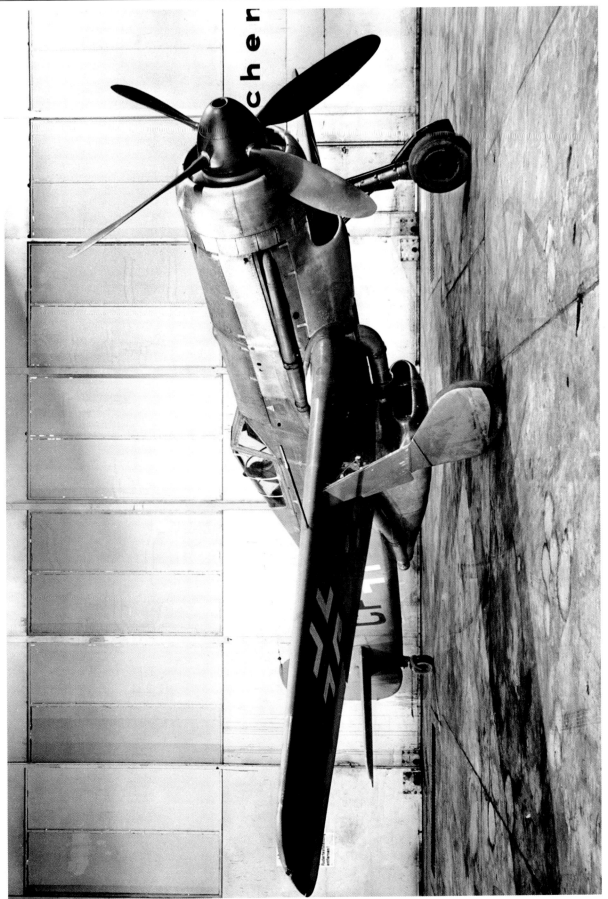

Fw 190 CF+OY with Hirth turbosupercharger and ventral radiator. This was a difficult aircraft to fly, even for the experienced Rechlin test pilot Beauvais.

mendous thump, like when an automobile drives over a bump at high speed. After landing no damage was found on the aircraft. All that was left of the fuel tank was the main bulkhead and the mount. It looked as if the air pressure had forced the tank from the brackets and turned it sideways, after which it had broken away on both sides of the bulkhead."

The experiences of Beauvais and his comrades would fill a book, but unfortunately there is not space for them here. Flying the Fw 190 and later the Ta 152, he participated in the switch from radial engines to liquid-cooled power plants with two-stage superchargers. These machines proved superior to the Mustang and Thunderbolt in some respects. Beauvais also had many experiences flying the Fw 190 D and the Ta 152.

Fw 190 D-9, WNr. 210051.

Comparative Flights 190 - 109

Report by *Hauptmann* Gollob on the comparative flights between the Messerschmitt Bf 109 F-4 and the Focke-Wulf Fw 190 A-2 at Rechlin.

Copy

Hptm. Gollob   Rechlin, 10 Dec. 1941
Luftwaffe Test Stations Command   15023/41 Secret

Secret Command Matter

Report on the Comparative Flights
between Bf 109 F-4 (DB 601 E) and Fw 190 A-1/2 (BMW 801 C)

Production aircraft at full operational weight (armed) were used for the comparison. The experiences of JG 26 were considered in all comparisons and proposed modifications.

ASSIGNMENT
1. Compare the performance of the two types with particular emphasis on aspects relating to combat tactics.

2. Assess the technical condition of the Fw 190 A-1/2 based on operational experience.

3. Suggest changes.

4. General assessment of the aircraft with respect to the proposed production program.

As to 1:
The comparative flights produced the following results:

a.) Speed
The Fw 190 A-2 is not as fast as the Bf 109 F-4. In practical terms, however, from an operational point of view it should be considered equally fast. The Fw 190 A-2's inferiority is more marked at higher altitudes, where it is 15 to 20 km/h slower, while it is almost as fast between 4000 and 4500 m.
At low altitude it is equally fast, or even about 10 km/h faster.

b.) Acceleration
Comparison at climb-combat power after 3 minutes

At a height of 0050 m the Fw 190 A-2 is approx.	0 to 500 m ahead
At a height of 2000 m the Fw 190 A-2 is approx.	100 to 200 m behind
At a height of 4000 m the Fw 190 A-2 is approx.	50 to 100 m behind
At a height of 6000 m the Fw 190 A-2 is approx.	200 to 250 m behind
At a height of 8000 m the Fw 190 A-2 is approx.	250 to 300 m behind
At a height of 10000 m the Fw 190 A-2 is approx.	400 to 600 m behind

Takeoff – emergency power produced the same picture. The Fw 190 A-2's inferior acceleration in level flight became evident during the comparison.

c.) Dive

The comparison was flown at combat power, approximately 20% dive and a height difference of 2000 m. The result was a lead of several hundred at all altitudes by the Fw 190 A-2. The steeper and longer the dive, the greater the lead. The tests did show, however, that the Fw 190 A-2 took longer to reach its maximum speed than the Bf 109 F-4.

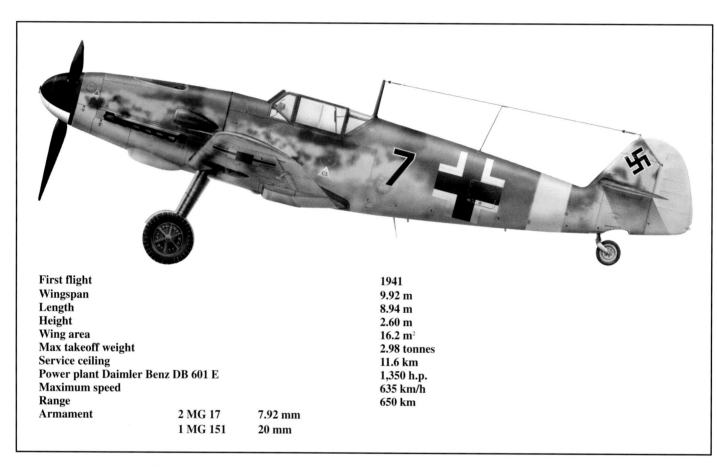

First flight	1941
Wingspan	9.92 m
Length	8.94 m
Height	2.60 m
Wing area	16.2 m²
Max takeoff weight	2.98 tonnes
Service ceiling	11.6 km
Power plant Daimler Benz DB 601 E	1,350 h.p.
Maximum speed	635 km/h
Range	650 km

Armament	2 MG 17	7.92 mm
	1 MG 151	20 mm

d.) Climb

The Fw 190 A-2 is much inferior in the climb, as the following comparison shows.

Time to climb from	Fw 190 A-2	Bf 109 F-4
1000 – 5000 m	4 min., 50 sec.	4 min.
1000 – 10000 m	18 min., 50 sec.	12 min., 30 sec.

The Fw 190 A-2's time to climb from 1000 to 10000 meters is thus six minutes longer than that of the Bf 109 F-4. This represents roughly a 50% poorer performance than the Bf 109 F-4.

e.) Control Forces, Turns

The Fw 190 A-2's control forces were rated as low. Even at 700 km/h, the aircraft can be flown with acceptable control forces, unlike the Bf 109 F-4. Maneuverability is good, and noticeably superior to that of the Bf 109 F-4, especially in reversals and at higher speeds. The Fw 190 A-2's rolling ability represents a significant advance, which will have positive effects in aerial combat. It has yet to be determined whether the Fw 190 turns tighter than the Bf 109.

f.) Takeoff and Landing Characteristics
The Fw 190's takeoff distance is about 60 to 70 meters greater on account of its higher weight. For the same reason, landing speed is about 15 km/h higher. The Fw 190's robust construction (undercarriage) and its superior stability at low speeds (no tendency to ground loop or drop a wing) make it possible for the Fw 190 A-2 to land in just as short a distance as the Bf 109 F-4, however. Slightly too much or too little speed on approach has a much greater effect on sink rate than with the Bf 109 F-4. In one case the aircraft drops sharply, in the other the landing run is increased considerably. There is no tendency to swing on landing. Of particular significance, belly landings result in little damage, with no distortion of the wings or fuselage, which almost always happens with the Bf 109. This contributes to the large number of Bf 109s written off.

g.) View from the Cockpit:
Forward good, but strongly dependent on the condition of the windscreen. Contamination by oil or other substances has a much more negative effect on visibility with the steeply-sloped windscreen than on the more vertical windscreen of the Bf 109. View to the rear is superior to that of the Bf 109. View for takeoff and landing is poorer than in the Bf 109.

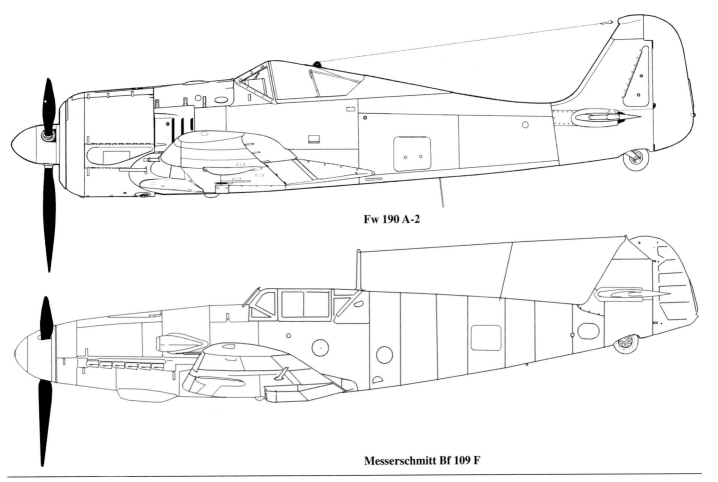

Fw 190 A-2

Messerschmitt Bf 109 F

As to 2.

a.) structural Strength of the Fw 190:
It is sufficient for all stresses encountered in combat. There is, however, no reason to assume that structural strengthening will be required at a later date like the Bf 109. Even lowering the undercarriage at high speed does not result in particular difficulties or other consequences.

b.) Power Plant Fw 190:
Based on experience to date, the engine must be characterized as unreliable and not ready for front-line service. The average operating duration has just the 25-hour mark. At present about 20 modifications have to be carried out on the engines. Consequently, until the engine can be brought to the level of operating reliability of the DB 601 E, the aircraft can only be characterized as conditionally fit for service. The reduced vulnerability of the air-cooled radial engine to combat damage has already been demonstrated in action.

As to 3.

Fw 190:
Concerning modifications to the engine, these are already contained in a summary by JG 26, likewise in general the modifications affecting the engine control device (Kommandogerät). Therefore, the following only makes reference to those modifications which appear necessary and which are not known to have been identified or addressed.

Airframe: The elevators must be fitted with grip-proof tips. The mounting of these and the ailerons must be carried out with great care, as faulty mounting will have a very unfavorable influence on handling characteristics. Therefore more care must be required of the factory pilots when test-flying the aircraft, as the units lack the experience to correct the very sensitive ailerons. Improper setting of the ailerons or unequal mounting of the tips results in aileron vibration at certain speeds and leads to premature stalling in turns.

Undercarriage:
At higher speeds after takeoff the undercarriage retracts poorly and slowly. JG 26 has therefore proposed that the undercarriage motor be replaced by a smaller electric motor plus hydraulics, which will completely eliminate this shortcoming. The best solution, however, would be direct connection of the hydraulics to the motor.

Pilot's Seat:
The cockpit is too narrow. The explosive canopy jettison system is viewed as not reliable. It is proposed that a mechanical jettisoning system be adopted. Cockpit ventilation must be improved significantly. Temperatures of up to 45 degrees were registered in summer; the pilot's ability to perform is seriously reduced even at 30 degrees. Such high temperatures also increase the incidence of illnesses in pilots (rheumatism, colds), especially in summer.

Head Armor:

The sloped position is unsuitable. The head armor must be mounted vertically, approximately as an extension of the back armor. Focke-Wulf has received JG 26's proposal.

Fouling of the Windscreen:

JG 26 has come up with an aerodynamic seal and oil collector in the gearing, and furthermore, by adding three holes in the propeller spinner mounting ring, has on sured that oil seeping from the propeller is blown into the engine. It is proposed that the manufacturer adopt this solution.

Weapons:

There must be a complete counter mechanism for all six weapons. The firing lever on the new stick grip with weapons selector switch is much too far away and must be moved onto the grip in a position approximating that of the firing lever on the old stick grip from where it can be operated comfortably with the index finger without loosening the grip on the stick. A request is being formulated that, while simultaneously firing the four central weapons, the pilot be able to select the wing cannon separately as desired. For tactical reasons, therefore, a separate firing button is required for the wing cannon (outer), because it is the most convenient for this purpose and can also be used, somewhat rarely, as a bomb-release button. As there is no requirement to fire less than four weapons at one time (four central weapons), the entire weapons selector would become unnecessary. The centralized mounting of two MG 151s and two MG 17s is extremely advantageous, and its has been found that the synchronization of the MG 151s functions flawlessly. No tests were carried out to determine the effect on climbing performance of installing two MG 151 or MG FF cannon in the wings. An increase of 0.5 to 1 minute in time to climb to 10000 meters can probably be expected.

Other:

The circuit breaker panel is poorly designed, because one
1. has to lift the cover to operate the buttons,
2. cannot clearly see the selector buttons while sitting in a normal position, as they are located too deep in the box. It is necessary that all the circuit-breaker buttons be affixed to the exterior of the circuit breaker panel with labels beside them, as in the Bf 109. At present it is not possible to see and select the desired switch quickly. The cover, which is kept closed by spring pressure, is uncomfortable and unnecessary.

Trimming:

At present the electric trim is operated by a toggle switch, which is very small and almost level with the cover panel. It must be possible to operate the trim control at any time, while eliminating possible selection errors. It is therefore necessary to significantly increase the size of the toggle switch so that it projects at least 1 to 1.5 cm above the casing.

Throttle Lever:

The throttle lever arm, which is curved toward the rear, must be lengthened so that it can be operated comfortably by the pilot, even in the full throttle position.

As to 4:

The following considerations have been put forward concerning the proposed production ration of Fw 190 to Bf 109.

At the present time the engine is so unreliable that, in the opinion of *Oberst* Galland, the aircraft is only conditionally capable of operations, while operations over the sea to England are presently out of the question. According to the engine experts, it will be at least half a year before the BMW 801 C and D engines will not be fit for operational use, like the DB 601 E, and then only after numerous changes (already 20).

It cannot be assumed that an air-cooled engine in the 2,000-h.p. class will be available for service use in the distant future. Developments in enemy aircraft will probably force us to turn to powerful liquid-cooled engines, in spite of the great advantages of air-cooled types.

It is intended that the liquid-cooled DB 603 will follow the BMW 801 D as a power plant for the Fw 190. It must be said that the DB 603 is also a completely new engine which will have its teething troubles. This engine should not be expected to reach the front in less than a year, by which time the BMW 801 will just have reached a suitable level of operational reliability. Today the BMW 801 C engine is averaging just 25 hours of operation.

The Fw 190's technical problems will thus continue for a considerable time, during which the only really suitable front-line fighter aircraft will be the Bf 109 F-4 or G (with developed engine). The installation of the BMW 801 C or D should only be viewed as an interim solution, which is confirmed by the next installation plans.

Equally as uncertain as operations over the Channel, are those over other bodies of water or over Russia. The makeup of our pilots today is such that losses due to mechanical problems cannot be accepted.

Employment of the Fw 190 in the tropics will result in greater engine problems, thereby limiting its use. As long as the BMW 801 lasts for so few operating hours, still far short of 50 hours of operation, numerous engines will have to be provided as replacements. This will run into difficulties as soon as several units convert to the Fw 190.

The planned production ratio of roughly 50% Fw 190s and 50% Bf 109s suggests that other units will convert soon. Once this happens, these units can only be deployed over our own territory, and either the engine problems will have to be cured by then or provisions will have to be made for frequent engine changes, neither of which can be expected. Development also clearly shows that the Bf 109 will always be faster and have a better climb rate than the Fw 190. Rate of climb is vital, however. Even if the Fw 190 suffices at the moment, given the nature of operations on the Channel, or does not play a major role, one cannot overlook its inferiority with the BMW 801 C compared to the Bf 109 F-4, which takes half as long as the Fw 190 to climb to 10000 meters. With the BMW 801 D this inferiority will still be on the order of 25 to 30 percent the climb performance of the Bf 109 F-4.

In view of these considerations, the ratio of 50% for the Fw 190 seems to have been set too high, even considering the greater vulnerability to battle damage of the Bf 109.

Signed Gollob
Rechlin, 6 Jan. 1942

Fw 190 V1 with BMW 139, first flight on 1 June 1939.

V2 with BMW 139, WNr. 0 002, RM+CB, with NACA cowling.

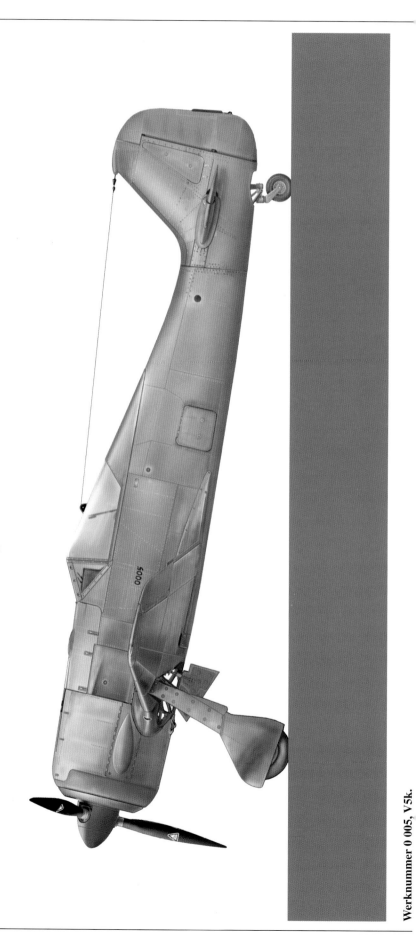

Werknummer 0 005, V5k.

Werknummer 0 022, SB+IB, first flight summer 1941. As the A-0/U4 it was used for engine trials and tests with external stores.

Fw 190 A-0 SB+KA / Fw 190 A-1 Ti+lK

Fw 190 A-0, manufacturer's code SB+KA, on the airfield in Bremen. (Colorized photograph)

Werknummer 0 046, TI+IK. This A-1 was later modified to serve as a prototype for a high-altitude fighter. As the B-0 it first flew in early 1943, powered by a BMW 801 D engine with a wing area of 20.3 m².

A Fw 190 Aa-3 of the Turkish Air Force.

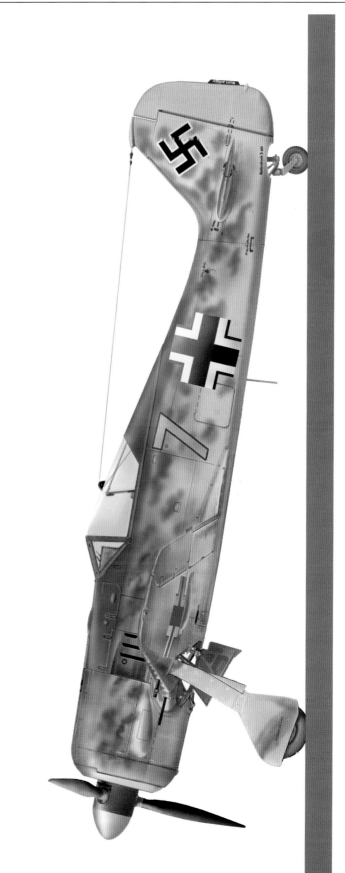

Fw 190 A-3, "Yellow 7", of 12./JG 5. This was Ernst Scheufele's usual aircraft in Norway in 1942.

A-5/U14 armed with the BT 1400 carried on an ETC 502 rack, as flown at Hexengrunde.

A-5/U14 with BT 1400.

The Aviation Museum in Hanover-Laatzen: the only Fw 190 in a German museum. Not to be overlooked is the BMW 801 engine next to the aircraft. Many original parts were used in restoring both the aircraft and engine.

The Fw 190 Heute

The Fw 190 A-8/N takes shape.

Whether it is the instrument panel in the **interior** of the gray-painted cockpit or the fuselage with **character**istic engine cowling, the wings and tail surfaces; everything is exactly like the original.

The exterior finish is of particular importance to a convincing overall effect. The horizontal tail surfaces in the foreground have received a coat of primer. The elevators still have to receive their fabric covering, which will then be painted.

Production Begins
The Pre-Production Series

Once the RLM issued a contract for a pre-production series, Focke-Wulf began preparations to build the Fw 190 A-0 series in Bremen. The number of aircraft specified in the contract was 20, and this was later increased to 28. The first Fw 190 pre-production aircraft were assigned the serial numbers 0 008 to 0 035. The purpose of the pre-production series was to make the Fw 190 ready for front-line service. From the beginning, therefore, Focke-Wulf equipped these Fw 190s with various versions of the BMW 801 engine and a variety of armament combinations and radio equipment. The Fw 190 V5 and V6 prototypes were also included in the test series. The various Fw 190 equipment packages were designated conversion sets, which were identified by the U suffix plus a number (U3, for example).

The various planned equipment states for the Fw 190 A-0 went from the Fw 190 A-0/U1 to the Fw 190 A-0/U13 (see table). Not all of the planned conversion sets were realized, for example the Fw 190 V11 as the Fw 190 A-0/U6 with an

A Fw 190 A-0 (V5g) is towed into position for takeoff.

Focke-Wulf
Flugzeugbau G.m.b.H.

Geheim!

Ändrg. Datum: 4.12.42 | 16.3.43 | 29.5.43

Fw 190 A	Werk-Nr.	Triebwerk	Schußwaffe Rumpf	Schußwaffe Flügel i.	Schußwaffe Flügel a.	Abwurfw./Zusatzbeh. Rumpf	Abwurfw./Zusatzbeh. Fläche	FT-Anlage	Bemerkungen	Bezchng.	Flugzeuge Stck. Auslieferg.	Abnehmer	Musterprüfung	Verwendung
A-0	0008+35	BMW 801 C/D	2 MG 17	2 MG 17	2 MG FF			FuG VIIa	O-Serie	Jäger		RLM	V5g+k	Jäger
A-0/U-1	0005 u. 0006	BMW 801C						=		=		RLM	V5g+k	Jäger
A-0/U-2	0008 10,12,13	=	2 MG 17	2 MG 131				=	1.10.41 Bruch	=		RLM	V5g+k	Jäger
A-0/U-3	21	=						FuG VIIa FuG 25	Werk-Nr. 0023 i. Rechlin FT-Träger	=		RLM	V5g+k	Jäger
A-0/U-4	0022,23	=	2 MG17	2 MG 17	2 MG FF	(500 kg) (300 ltr.)	2×250 kg 2×300 ltr.	FuG VIIa	Waffenträger MG 151 Erprobung	=		RLM	V5g+k	Jäger
A-0/U-5	0018	BMW 801 C-1	2 MG 17	2 MG 151	"			FuG VIIa	Gurt FF-Erprobung	=		RLM	V5g+k	Jäger
A-0/U-10	0030	=	MG17	2 MG 17	2 MG FF-G			FuG VII		=		RLM	V5g+k	Jäger
A-0/U-11	0015	"	"	"	2 MG FF			FuG VII	GM-I Erprobung Rüstsatz	=		RLM	V5g+k	Jäger
A-0/U-12	0031	BMW 801D	=	"	"			=	Motorerprobungsträger D-Motor	=		RLM	V5g+k	Jäger
A-0/U-13	0025+28	BMW 801D	=	"	"							RLM	V5g+k	Jäger
A-1	190.0110 001+102	BMW 801 C-1	2 MG17	2 MG 17	2 MG FF	(500 kg) (250 kg) (300 ltr.)		FuG VII FuG 25	Bomben u. Reichweite Reichweite a. ER_1-Pumpe	Jäger	102 Serie 6.41 + 1.42	RLM	V7	Jäger
A-1/U-1		BMW 801 D	=	"	"	o		=	D-statt C-Motor	=		RLM	V7	Jäger

This extract from the Focke-Wulf production list provides a good overview of the equipment installed in the various pre-production aircraft.

WNr. 016.

WNr. 016 on the company airfield in Bremen.

Fw 190 A-0: pre-production aircraft in the company hangar.

Servicing the engine of the Fw 190 A-0/
U11, KB+PQ, WNr. 0 015.

Visible beyond the A-0/U11 (WNr. 0
015) are KB+PJ, an A-1; another A-0;
and A-1 WNr. 0 012, KB+PN.

A-0/U11, KB+PQ, WNr. 0 015; two A-
0s and another Fw 190. Just visible on
the right is a Fw 191.

Above: The first A-0s went straight into testing without first being painted in camouflage. In the foreground is WNr. 0 010, an A-0/U2 with the small wing. The lettering on the cowling indicates that the aircraft was powered by the improved BMW 801 C-1 engine. The aircraft's armament consisted of two MG 17s in the fuselage and two MG 131 machine-guns in the wing roots. Below: Fw 190 A-0, KB+PV, being refueled at Focke-Wulf's airfield in Bremen.

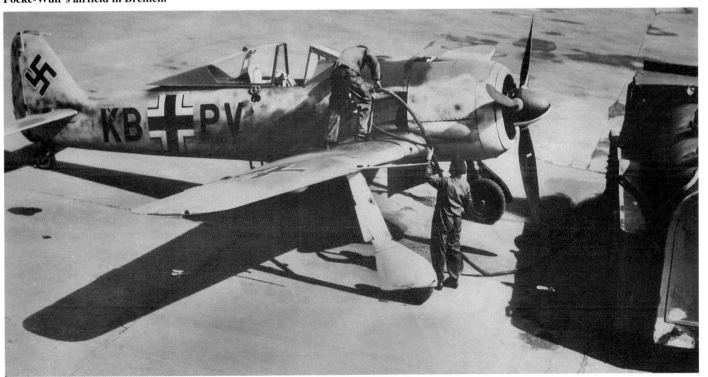

WNr. 0 020, KB+PV, in flight. These photographs were taken in 1942.

Fw 190 A-0, KB+PV, is prepared for a flight at Focke-Wulf's airfield in Bremen. The MG 17s in the fuselage and wing roots and the wing-mounted MG FF cannon have been sealed to prevent the entry of dust.

Fw 190 A-0. Working on the starboard main undercarriage leg.

Facing page:
Experts clustered about the engine compartment of KB+PS, an A-0, WNr. 0017.

American Wright radial engine. The A-0 series of experimental aircraft also included the first two Fw 190s equipped as fighter-bombers (*Werknummer* 0 022 and 0 025). These two machines, whose designation was Fw 190 A-0/U4, were capable of carrying two 250-kg bombs or two 300-liter drop tanks beneath the outer wings. *Werknummer* 0 031 was the first to employ the GM 1 power boost system and was designated the Fw 190 A-0/U12. In addition to the planned standard armament of four MG 17 machine-guns and two MG

FF cannon, four aircraft were built as the Fw 190 A-0/U2 with MG 131 machine-guns in the wing roots. The MG 151 also fit in the wing roots of the Fw 190. The first aircraft so equipped was the Fw 190 A-0/U5, *Werknummer* 0 018. Focke-Wulf issued ready-to-fly dates for the first twelve pre-production machines at the end of 1939, however the third A-0 was delivered in February 1941. At the beginning of 1941 the first three Fw 190 A-0s (WNr. 0 011, 0 016 and 0 018) underwent intensive testing at Focke-Wulf's Bremen factory.

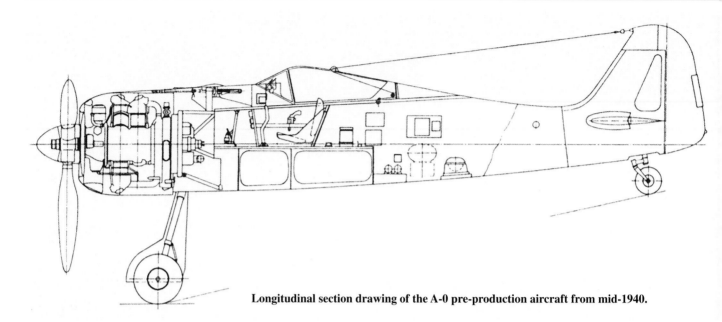

Longitudinal section drawing of the A-0 pre-production aircraft from mid-1940.

By that time the V6 had already made 22 flights. *Werknummer* 0 018 made twelve flights at that time and 0 016 thirteen. In February 1944, 0 017 and 0 020 began leaking oil. 0 017 subsequently received a new BMW 801 A which had been converted into a BMW 801 D. The aircraft joined the test program in May 1941 together with three other A-0s. Six more followed in June, one in July, one in August, two in September and one in October, bringing the total number of aircraft to 18. Construction of Fw 190 A-1 and A-2 began while the Fw 190 A-0 pre-production aircraft were still being built. The RLM usually insisted that a new aircraft complete the testing phase before issuing a production contract, however it took a big risk with the Fw 190. In contrast to similar cases, the He 177 for example, the risk paid off. The first four Fw 190 A-1s

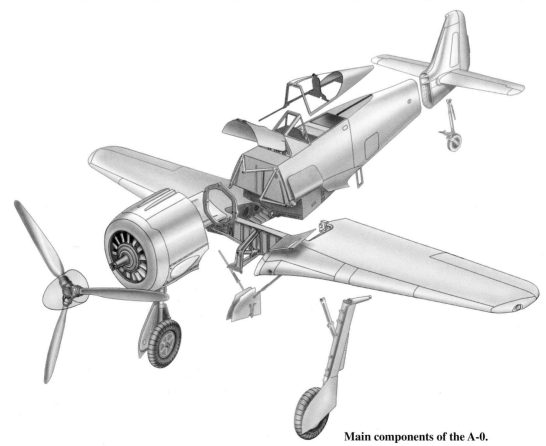

Main components of the A-0.

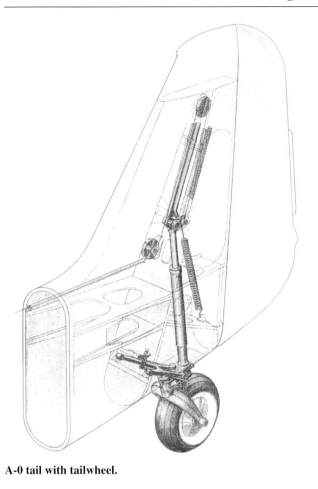

A-0 tail with tailwheel.

A-0, tail, WNr. 0 034.

Tail section of the A-0/U2/U13, WNr. 0 014.

Close-up of the engine cowling of WNr. 0 013, an A-0/U2, KB+PO.

left the Bremen factory in June 1941, followed in mid-1941 by the first Fw 190 A-2s built by Arado in Warnemünde. By the end of 1942 Focke-Wulf had completed 18 A-0 pre-pro-

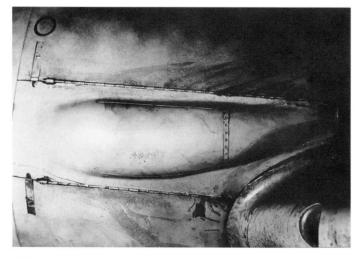

WNr. 0 014 was equipped with a BMW 801 D engine. The adoption of the new engine made it necessary to revise the shape of the bulged fairing over the cooling intake bypass duct.

duction aircraft, 96 A-1s and 16 A-2s, Arado 15 A-2s and AGO 17 A-2s.

In March 1941 a Fw 190 test detachment was formed in Rechlin to assist in readying the Fw 190 for service use. This test unit was assigned a variety of pre-production aircraft and prototypes. In the 23rd and 24th weeks of 1941, for example, it received A-0s 0017, 0024, 0026 and 0027, plus two A-1 production aircraft, 001 and 003. *Werknummer* 016, which had been received earlier, was used to make a high-altitude flight to 9000 meters. The test detachment was based at Roggentin in Mecklenburg and its personnel included a number of experienced *Luftwaffe* officers. JG 26 *Schlageter* had been selected as the first unit to receive the Fw 190, and it sent a detachment of 30 personnel under the command of *Oberleutnant* Otto Behrens of 6. *Staffel* and technical officer *Oberleutnant* Karl Borris. Focke-Wulf supported the detachment with experienced engineers and technicians. Tank's co-worker and friend Johannes "Spez" Krammel maintained contact between the detachment and Focke-Wulf. Krammel assisted the units when later variants of the Fw 190 were in-

The starboard engine cowling of WNr. 0 014, revealing the exhaust vents typical of the A-2 series.

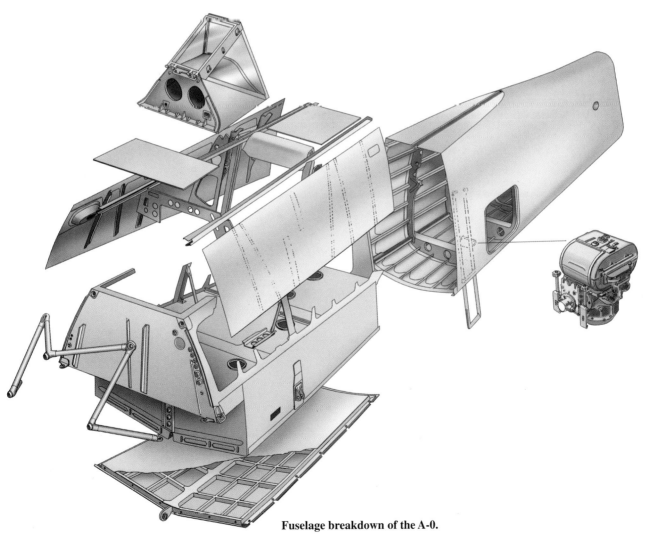

Fuselage breakdown of the A-0.

Flugklar-Termine Fw 190					
Werk-Nummer	0 005	15.5.1940	Werk-Nummer	0 013	16.9.1940
Werk-Nummer	0 006	31.5.1940	Werk-Nummer	0 014	24.09.1940
Werk-Nummer	0 008	20.7.1940	Werk-Nummer	0 015	02.10.1940
Werk-Nummer	0 009	6.8.1940	Werk-Nummer	0 016	10.10.1940
Werk-Nummer	0 010	22.8.1940	Werk-Nummer	0 017	18.10.1940
Werk-Nummer	0 011	30.08.1940	Werk-Nummer	0 018	26.10.1940
Werk-Nummer	0 012	7.9.1940	Werk-Nummer	0 019	4.11.1940
			Werk-Nummer	0 020	12.11.1940

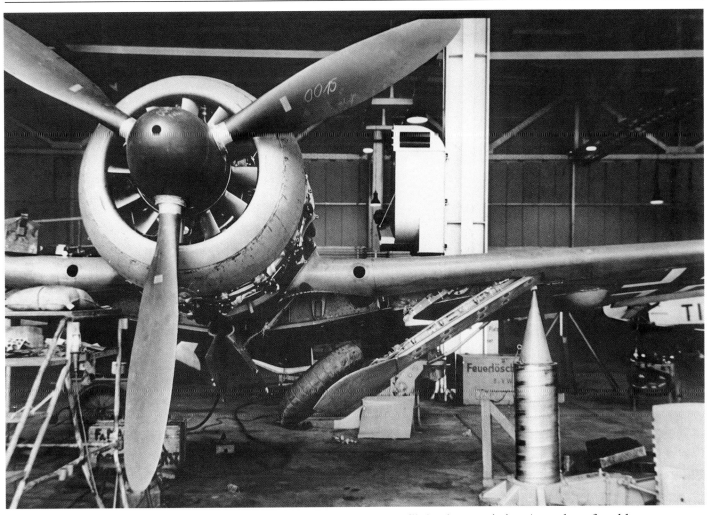

troduced, serving as a fitter-engineer. There were numerous hurdles to get over before the aircraft entered service, however. Even Prof. Kurt Tank and Oberingenieur Käether assisted the test detachment in every possible respect. They were determined that the Fw 190 should be a success.

The test pilots and pilots of JG 26 tested the new Fw 190 fighter hard, in order to discover any shortcomings in its de-

sign or flight characteristics. A number of problems were encountered during the test phase, problems which every new aircraft encountered, especially one with a brand new engine. While the pilots were enthusiastic about the Fw 190's handling characteristics from the very beginning, the new BMW 801 engine proved a source of trouble. Oil and fuel lines broke, the annular oil cooler cracked and engine cooling was still

Above: WNr. 0015, KB+PQ, was an A-0/U11.

Facing page, top: MG 17 installation in the upper fuselage of the A-0.

Facing page, center: Focke-Wulf schedule for the first flights of the pre-production aircraft, dated 23 December 1939.

Facing page, bottom: The fuselage weapons installation of A-0, WNr. 0 009. The cockpit fresh air intake is situated between the two machine-gun barrels.

Right: The MG FF 20-mm cannon, weight 26.3 kg. Focke-Wulf first tested this cannon in the outer wing position of the pre-production series. The weapon was built under license from Oerlikon, Switzerland.

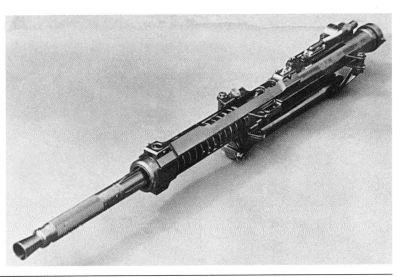

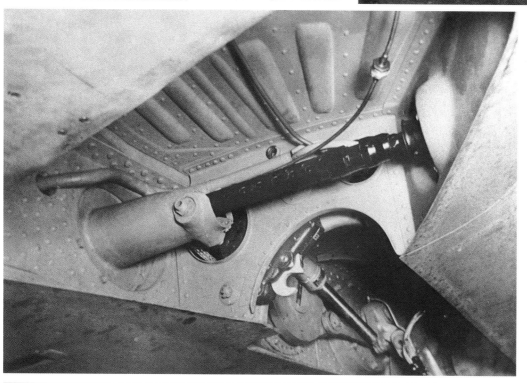

Above left, right: The MG FF cannon with belt feed in the outer wing of WNr. 0030, SB+IJ. For weapons trials the A-0/U10 was armed with two MG 17 machineguns in the fuselage, two MG 151 cannon in the wing roots, and two MG FF cannon in the outer wings.

Left: MG 17 machine-gun in the wing root of an A-0.

Wheel well door of the A-0/U2.

KB+PQ, WNr. 0 015.

MG 131 machine-gun in the wing root of an A-0. This 13-mm weapon weighed 20.5 kg, with a length of 1168 mm. Its projectiles weighed 34 g.

Above: The barrel of the Rheinmetall MG 131 machine-gun in the undercarriage bay of an A-0. Opposite: KB+PU, WNr. 0019, on jacks in the prototype shop for weapons alignment. Powered by the BMW 801 C-0 and C1, by 30 June 1941 this machine logged nine hours in 32 flights.

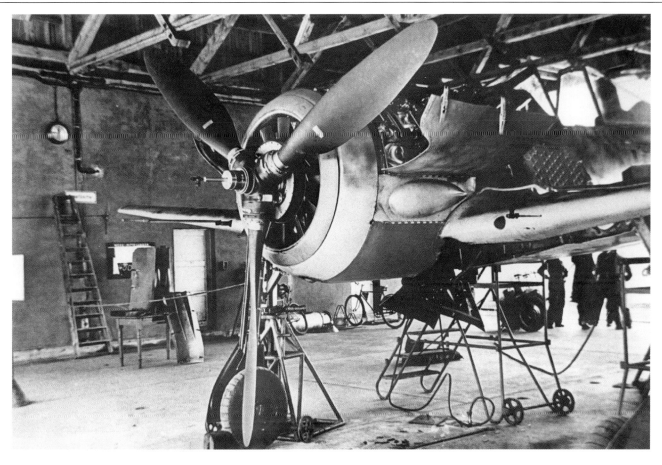

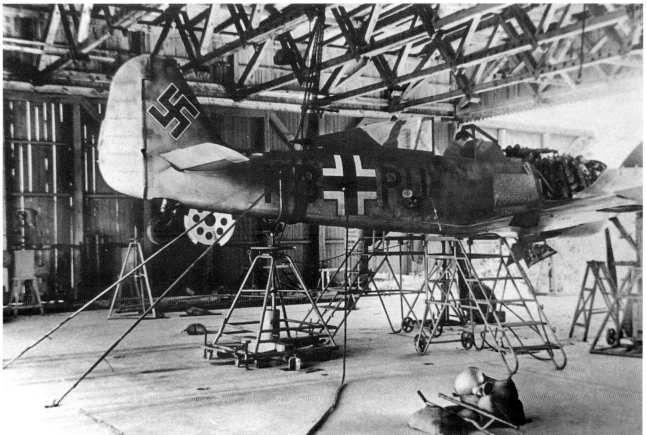

A-0 on jacks for weapons tests. Baskets have been placed beneath the shell casing ejector chutes.

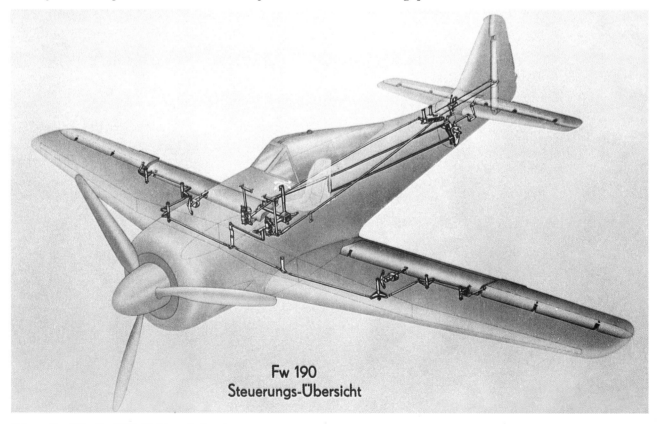

Fw 190
Steuerungs-Übersicht

Schematic of the Fw 190's flight control system.

The Fw 190 V5k; the A-0/U4, WNr. 0 019, KB+PU; and another A-0 during an engine run-up.

A Fw 190 A-0.

WNr. 0 021, SB+IA, is prepared for a flight.

The Fw 190 V8, WNr. 0 021, was flown with improved radio equipment consisting of an FuG VIIa and a FuG 25.

The Fw 190 V8, an A-0/U4, WNr. 0 021, manufacturer's code SB+IA, made its first flight in early 1941. The V8 was powered by a BMW 801 C-0. armament consisted of four MG 17 machine-guns and two MG FF cannon in the outer wings. It was lost in a crash on 1 October 1941.

The Fw 190 V9 A0/U4, WNr. 0 022, manufacturer's code SB+IB, first flew in mid-1941. It was used to test the Fw 190 in the fighter-bomber role. Here an SC 250 practice bomb is mounted on the ETC rack beneath the fuselage.

The Fw 190 V9, an A-0/U4, WNr. 0 022, manufacturer's code SB+IB, with a 300-liter drop tank on the fuselage rack.

The Fw 190 V9 carrying an SC 250 practice bomb.

WNr. 0 022 is prepared for a test flight with a practice bomb.

The Fw 190 A0/U4, WNr. 0 022, manufacturer's code SB+IB, was used for numerous experiments and test flights with bombs and external tanks. Designated the V9, it first flew in early 1941, powered by a BMW 801 C-0 engine. According to BMW records, the aircraft logged 11 flying hours in 21 flights by 30 June 1941. Improved BMW 801 C-1 and D engines were later installed. This photo shows the aircraft being refueled. Note the 300-l drop tank on the ETC 501 rack.

The revised shape of the armored nose ring and upper engine cowling are clearly visible on the Fw 190 V9, WNr. 0 022.

Carrying an SC 250.

300-liter drop tank.

Left: WNr. 0023, manufacturer's code SB+IC, was tested at Rechlin with bombs and external tanks.

These two photographs depict a 300-liter external tank on an experimental Focke-Wulf rack mounted on WNr. 0 022 or 0 023.

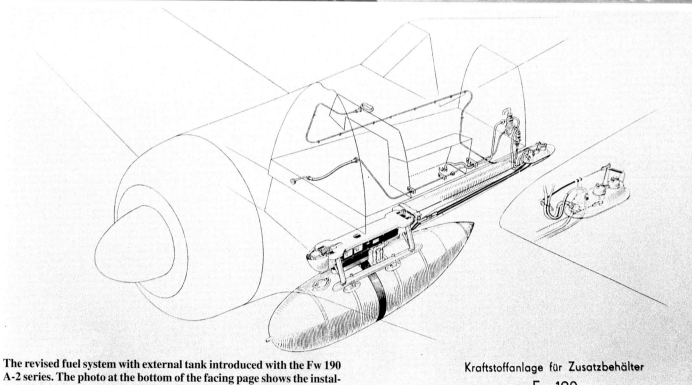

The revised fuel system with external tank introduced with the Fw 190 A-2 series. The photo at the bottom of the facing page shows the installation of an external tank on an A-0 in the prototype shop.

Kraftstoffanlage für Zusatzbehälter
Fw 190

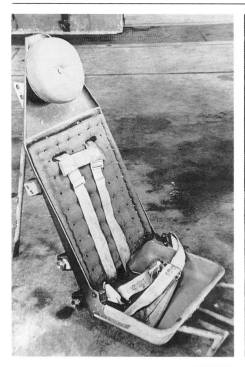 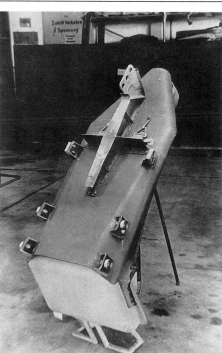 

The prototype ejector seat by Focke-Wulf. Tests were carried out with a wooden dummy in the seat. The cockpit of WNr. 0022 was modified to accept the seat. The escape system, which was powered by compressed air, was tested on the ground.

Fw 190 A-0, *Werknummer* 0 016, manufacturer's code KB+PS, was tested by Focke-Wulf with the BMW 801 C-0/C1 at the beginning of 1941. In the short period until 30 June 1941, two BMW 801 C-0 and two BMW 801 C-1 engines were flown in this aircraft. WNr. 0 016 went to Rechlin on 12 May 1941.

Fw 190 A-0, WNr. 0 024, SB+ID.

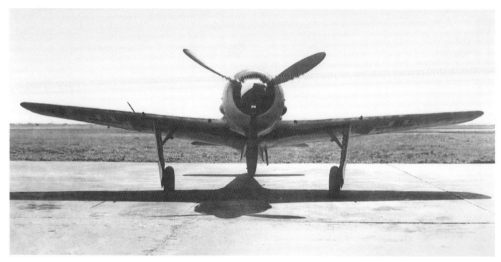

Fw 190 A-0. WNr. 0 024, SB+ID.

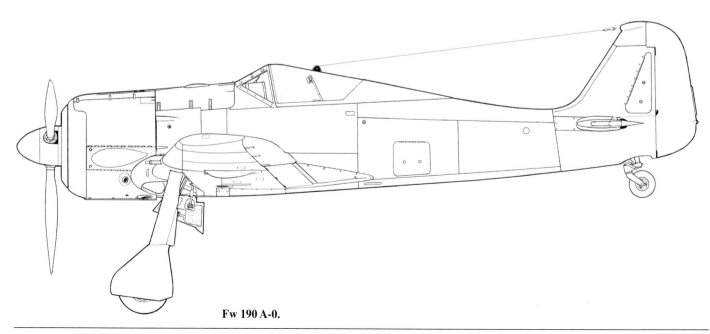

Fw 190 A-0.

Fw 190 A-0/U4, WNr. 0 024, manufacturer's code SB+ID.

A-0, WNr. 0 025, manufacturer's code SB+IE.

A-0, WNr. 0 027, manufacturer's code SB+IG. Parked on the right are two Fw 190 A-1/U1.

A-0, WNr. 0 027, manufacturer's code SB+IG.

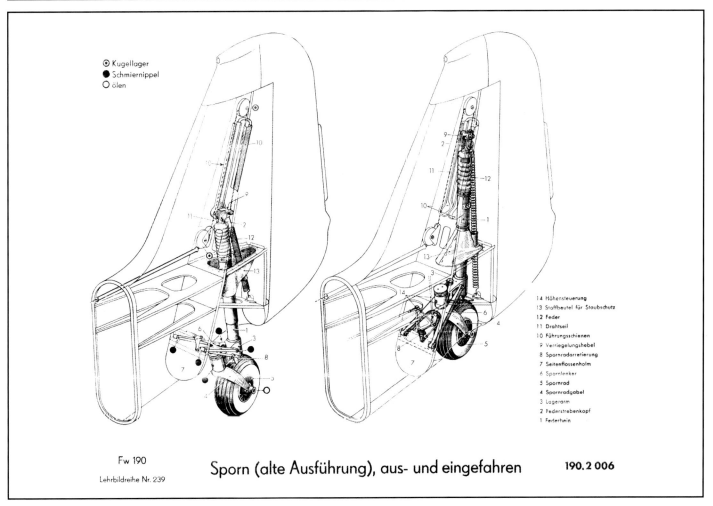

⊙ Kugellager
● Schmiernippel
○ ölen

14 Höhensteuerung
13 Staffbeutel für Staubschutz
12 Feder
11 Drahtseil
10 Führungsschienen
9 Verriegelungshebel
8 Spornradarretierung
7 Seitenflossenholm
6 Spornlenker
5 Spornrad
4 Spornradgabel
3 Lagerarm
2 Federstrebenkopf
1 Federbein

Fw 190
Lehrbildreihe Nr. 239

Sporn (alte Ausführung), aus- und eingefahren

190.2 006

Tailwheel (early version), extended and retracted.

A-0, WNr. 0027, manufacturer's code SB+IG, photographed prior to conversion to A-0/U13 standard.

A-0, WNr. 0 028, manufacturer's code SB+IH.

inadequate, resulting in seized pistons. On a number of occasions, parts of the engine cowling came off during high-speed flight.

There were also problems with the new propeller pitch control system, which did not always function properly. The test detachment also took the opportunity to test the new Fw 190 against the Bf 109 and a captured Spitfire.

The Fw 190 proved itself clearly superior to both aircraft. Although it was not possible to immediately correct all the shortcomings and weaknesses identified in flight testing, at least they had been identified, allowing improvements to be introduced. EK 190 (Fw 190 Test Detachment) subsequently issued a report to Focke-Wulf and BMW with more than 50 proposals for eliminating the problems that had been

encountered. Despite these problems, the pilots of JG 26 had been impressed by the aircraft's handling characteristics: they wanted the Fw 190. Focke-Wulf took steps to concentrate its efforts in the factory. In April 1941 the company officially suspended work on the Fw 191 twin-engined bomber to concentrate on the Fw 190. The forces made available were to concentrate their efforts on preparing the Fw 190 for quantity production.

In mid-1941 the Fw 190 began armament trials in Tarnewitz. At least five Fw 190 A-0s were tested there. *Werknummer* 0 012, 0 020, 0 024, 0 026 and 0 027 are known to have been there in the 25th and 26th calendar months. While there, *Werknummer* 0 026 reached a height of 11000 meters. 0 012 later went to Rechlin, where it crashed on 20 January 1942.

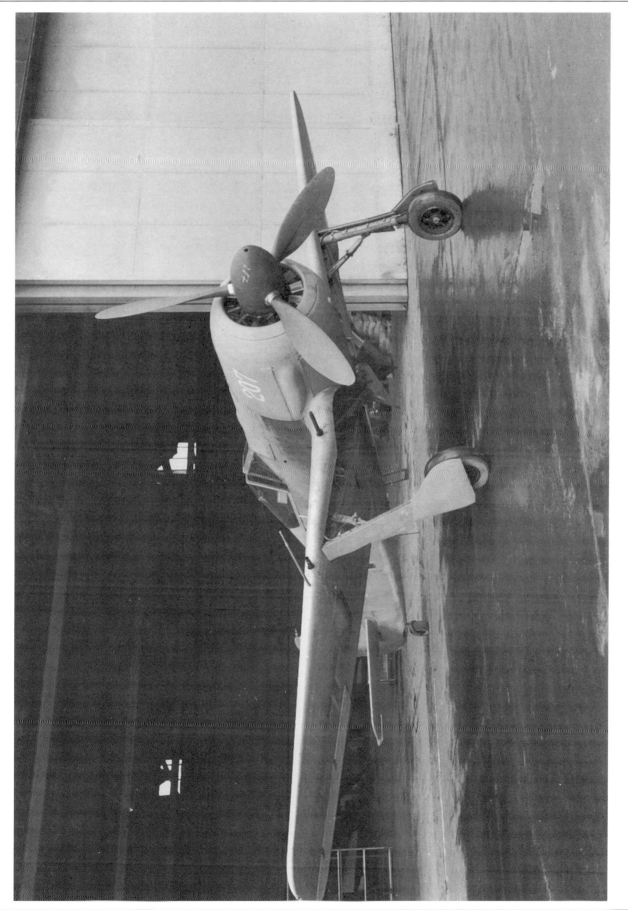

Werknummer 207, a Fw 190 A-2, was built by Arado in Warnemünde. 207 was completed in the 38th week of 1941 along with 204, 205, 206, 215 and 216. Armament consisted of two MG 17s in the fuselage, two MG 151s in the wing roots and two MG FF cannon in the outer wings. Power plant was the BMW 801 C.

The First Fw 190s in Service with JG 5

Memories of Fighter Pilot Ernst Scheufele

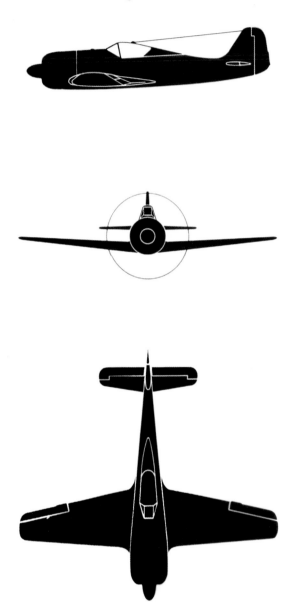

Three-view silhouette of the Fw 190 A. Right: Lt. Scheufele in 1943. Facing page: Top: Two Fw 190 A fighters in flight. Bottom: Mechanics work on the engine of a Fw 190 A-3. Norway, 1943.

JG 5 was deployed to Norway to protect German warships operating from there, defend airfields, submarine pens, ports and industrial facilities against attack by RAF bombers and attack British warships by day and night. The *Staffeln* of this unit received their first Fw 190s in the summer of 1942. The robust Fw 190 acquitted itself well in the difficult conditions, with frequent rain and fog and cold winter temperatures.

"In June 1942 I was transferred to the west coast of Norway. We flew the Me 109 E for one month, then in July the Me 109 F, and on 30 August 1942 we collected the first Focke-Wulf Fw 190s at Copenhagen-Vaerlöse."

The Fw 190s were initially operated from airfields at Örlandet, Trondheim and Bodö in southern and central Norway, but they later also flew from Banak and Alta in the north.

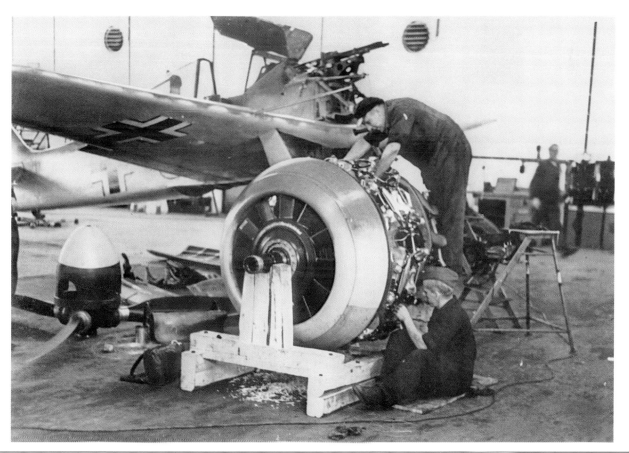

"They were the very first Fw 190s. I know the date so precisely because my friend Leutnant Heinz Löffler crashed while flying a Fw 190 in bad weather in Denmark. The aircraft was easy to fly. The electrical panel on the left side of the cockpit and, most important, the tailwheel lock after landing, were knew to us."

The Fw 190's electrical system gave the ground personnel additional problems in wet weather, which is common in Norway. Daily ground measurements on the aircraft were the rule, which, with the Fw 190, meant removing the pilot's seat to gain access to the battery. A short in the electrical system could result in retraction of the electrically-activated main undercarriage on the ground.

Ernst Scheufele in front of a brand-new Fw 190 A-2 with Oberfeldwebel Burckhardt, who joined the *Luftwaffe* in 1939. The propeller spinner and engine cowling are still in factory finish.

Fw 190 A-3 of 3./JG 5 in Norway at the end of 1942. "Yellow 2" is parked in front of a blast pen on the Herdla airfield. The maintenance personnel faced a difficult task in the extreme climatic conditions. Wearing the dark overhauls is Heinz Birkholz.

Leutnant Scheufele with his A-3 "Yellow 7" in Norway. Note the white tip of the propeller and the yellow cowling underside.

Ernst Scheufele posing on his Fw 190 A-3.

"The Me 109 had the unpleasant tendency to ground loop during the roll-out after landing. This usually resulted in damage to the propeller and wing.

Of course there was a very different feeling than in the more elegant Messerschmitt. My heart always dropped into my pants when the supercharger switched into high hear at a height of 3500 to 4000 meters. Each time it seemed as if the aircraft was coming apart.

When we arrived with the aircraft in Trondheim, *Oberleutnant* Huppert asked me to engage in mock combat with him in his Messerschmitt Bf 109. The Fw 190 and I were the clear losers. One reason was surely that he was the better flier; he already had the Knight's Cross and later received the Oak Leaves.

None of those who were there when the Fw 190 entered service with the *IV. Gruppe* of *Jagdgeschwader 5* are still alive. In our *12. Staffel* in Bodö we had both the 109 and Focke-Wulfs, side by side.

In 1943 we had the Focke-Wulf 190 A-2, A-3 and A-4. What we had in 1942, the first operational machines, I can no longer say with certainty."

The First Production Variants

Deliveries of the Fw 190 A-1, the first production version, began in June 1941. Production of the Fw 190 was expanded to licensed manufacturers. The first Fw 190 A-2 built by Arado in Warnemünde, WNr. 201, made its first flight on 22 July 1941. When production at Arado got into full swing, WNr. 201 went to Rechlin, while 202 went to Tarnewitz for further tests. Ago delivered its first Fw 190 A-2 in October 1941.

The first Fw 190 A-1 with the improved BMW 801 C-1 engine was received by *Jagdgeschwader 26* in August 1941.

Mass production of the Fw 190 begins. Shown here is the almost completed Fw 190 A-1/U1 with the WNr. 006.

Final assembly of Fw 190 A-1, WNr. 006.

During conversion to the Fw 190, the unit's pilots were enthusiastic about the type's flying qualities from the very outset. At that time the *Geschwader* was based at Paris-Le Bourget. Soon afterward it transferred to Moorseele in Belgium. Conversion training on the Fw 190 A-1 continued there with *Werknummer* 025 to 035. JG 26 and JG 2 were the only two fighter wings left in the west following the German attack on the Soviet Union. These two units were left to bear the brunt of Allied attacks in the west. The new fighter's baptism of fire came in September 1941, when Fw 190 A-1s of 6./JG 26 engaged a group of Spitfire Vs over Dunkirk. Three of the British fighters were shot down without loss. The Fw 190 A-1 was superior to the Spitfire Vb in almost every respect.

The superior performance of the Fw 190 enabled its pilots to break off combat whenever they wished. Despite improvements, the BMW 801 continued to give problems. It still had far to go to achieve practical operational maturity.

In 1941 it was still possible to conduct final assembly in the open air, as enemy aircraft were not yet a threat.

Engine problems kept serviceability levels low. In some cases faulty sparkplugs caused performance to fall off and caused engine vibration. There were also supercharger failures and fires in the engine compartment. Initial trials with the Fw 190 on the Eastern Front were no more successful.

The first operational trials by II./JG 54 in November 1944 began very poorly. The reasons for this were the hard Russian winter and the primitive maintenance facilities on the Eastern Front.

The infrastructure for the Fw 190 in the east was gradually improved, and the type served successfully there until the end of the war. The armament of the Fw 190 A-1, which consisted of four MG 17 machine-guns and two MG FF cannon in the outer wings, was viewed as inadequate by the units. Subsequent variants of the Fw 190 were designed with increasingly heavier armament.

A lineup of production A-1/U1 fighters at Marienburg. In the foreground is WNr. 008, followed by 014, 027, 012, 006 and 024.

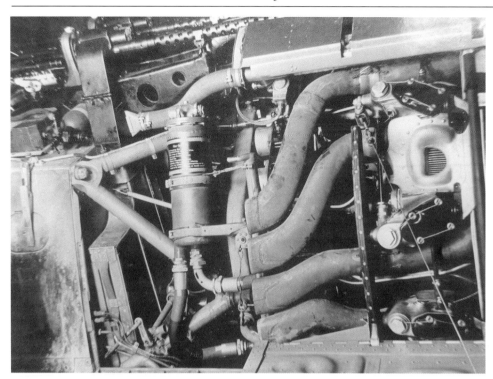

Close-up of the exhaust system and the engine bearer ring.

The MG 17 machine-guns and BMW 801 C engine as installed in a 190 A-0 pre-production machine. The armored oil cooler ring and the air intake fairing are clearly visible.

BMW 801 C-2.

This photograph shows the engine installed without cowling.

The first Fw 190 A-1s leave the Bremen plant. The engine of the aircraft in the foreground, WNr. 036, manufacturer's code TK+MJ, is already running.

Fw 190 A-1/U1, WNr. 001, manufacturer's code SB+KA.

Lineup of early production Fw 190 A-1s at Bremen. In the foreground is WNr. 036, manufacturer's code TK+MJ.

A-1/U1, SB+KP.

Focke-Wulf delivered 102 Fw 190 A-1 fighters to the *Luftwaffe* by January 1942. With a gross weight of 3900 kg, the Fw 190 A-1 achieved maximum speeds of 537 km/h at ground level and 676 km/h at an altitude of 6400 meters. It reached an altitude of 6000 meters in 7.9 minutes and had a

service ceiling of 10 600 m. Depending on equipment, the gross weight of the Fw 190 A-1 varied from 3660 to 4212 kg. The A-1s were assigned the *Werknummer* 110 001 to 110 102. *Werknummer* 110 001 was the first production Fw 190 with the improved BMW 801 C-1 engine. It was taken from pro-

This A-1, WNr. 016, manufacturer's code SB+KP, overturned on landing during flight trials.

Two more photos of the unfortunate SB+KP.

Pre-flight preparations by a Fw 190 A-1/U1, WNr. 067, manufacturer's code TI+DQ.

Company photo of Fw 190 A-1/U1, WNr. 001, manufacturer's code SB+KA.

Facing page:
Top: A-1 weapons installation.
Bottom: The undercarriage of the Fw 190 A-1.

Type Sheet Fw 190 A-1

Type	Fw 190
Wing area	18.3 m²
Wingspan	10.38 m
Maximum height	3.95 m
Maximum length	8.65 m
Power plant	BMW 801 C
Takeoff power	1,560 h.p. at 2,700 rpm at 0 m
	1,420 h.p. at 2,700 rpm at 5700 m
Propeller revolutions	1,290 rpm
Propeller	3-blade metal variable-pitch, D = 3.3 m

Performance at a Gross Weight of 3850 kg

Maximum speed at	height of	0 m	545 km/h
		1800 m	585 km/h
		3100 m	585 km/h
		5700 m	660 km/h
		8000 m	635 km/h
		10000 m	565 km/6
Rate of climb at ground level			16 m/sec
Time to climb to		2000 m	2.2 min
		4000 m	4.6 min
		6000 m	7.7 min
		8000 m	12 min
		10000 m	20.8 min
Service ceiling			11000 m
Takeoff distance			300 m
Landing speed			130 km/h
Range		at 5000 m	750 km

Additional Technical Information on the Fw 190 A-1

Undercarriage wheel track		3500 mm
Wheel diameter	Main undercarriage	700 x 175 mm
Electro-mechanically operated Tailwheel		350 x 135 mm
Fuel		524 liters (232 l in front tank, 292 liters in rear tank)
Oil		42 liters (max. 55 liters)
Power Plant		14-cylinder BMW 801 C air-cooled twin-row radial

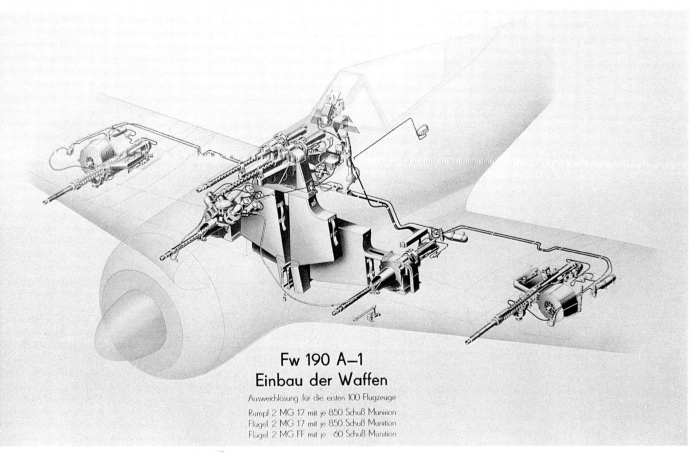

Fw 190 A–1
Einbau der Waffen
Ausweichlösung für die ersten 100 Flugzeuge
Rumpf 2 MG 17 mit je 850 Schuß Munition
Flügel 2 MG 17 mit je 850 Schuß Munition
Flügel 2 MG FF mit je 60 Schuß Munition

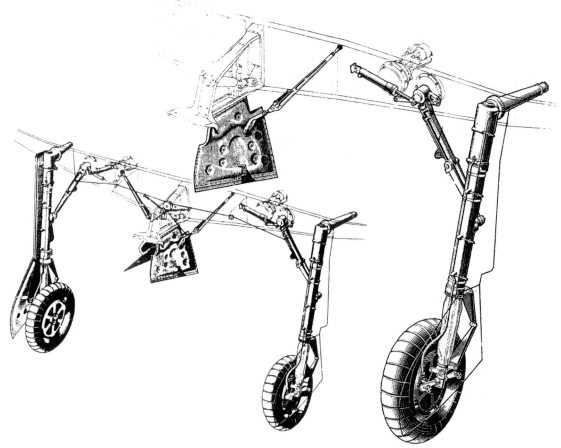

Cockpit of the A-1
1   Fine and coarse altimeter
2   Airspeed indicator
3   Turn and bank indicator
4   Vertical speed indicator
5   Boost pressure gauge
6   RPM indicator
7   Fuel and oil pressure gauge
8   Oil temperature gauge
9   Fuel contents gauge
10 Low fuel indicator lamp
11 Fuel contents gauge selector switch
12 Propeller pitch indicator
13 Oxygen flow meter
14 Oxygen pressure gauge
15 Oxygen dump valve
16 Tailplane incidence indicator
17 Junghans clock
18 Main instrument panel
19 Lower panel
20 Left console
21 Right console
22 Flare pistol mount
23 Flare box
24 Throttle lever and propeller pitch control

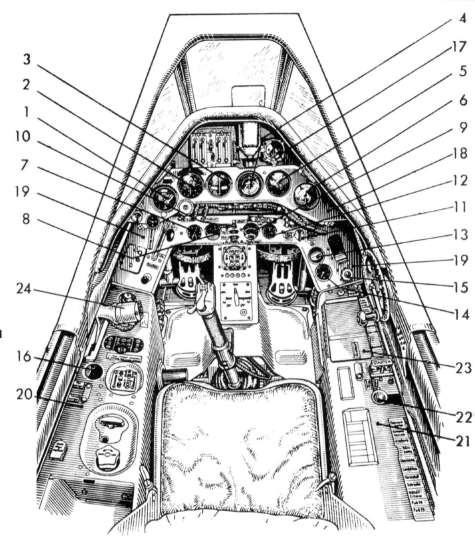

**Fw 190
Anordnung des Panzerschutzes**

Panzerringe um Ölkühler und Ölbehälter
Kopf-, Schulter- und Armschutz, Panzersitz
Beschußfeste Frontscheibe
Vollgeschützte Kraftstoffbehälter (mittelschwerer Schutz)

Arrangement of armor in the A-1.

Hans Sander in the cockpit of a Fw 190 A-1. This photo appeared as a retouched postcard on 1 June 1942. Title: Focke-Wulf Fw 190 fighter with BMW 801 twin-row radial engine.

This Focke-Wulf 190 A-1/U1, WNr. 100, was flown by Lt. H. Sternberg in the autumn of 1941.

Facing page:
Lt. Horst Sternberg of 5./JG 26 at scramble readiness. The Fw 190 A-1 sits in its blast pen, ready to take off.

Servicing an A-1. The most common cause of unserviceability was still the BMW 801 engine.

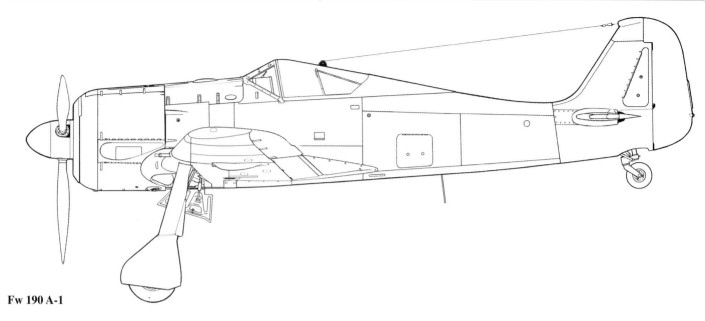

Fw 190 A-1

duction and was tested extensively by the company under the designation Fw 190 V7.

The next two production variants, the A-2 and A-3, were both fitted with heavier armament and more powerful engines. Both types carried two MG 151 cannon in the wing roots. The A-2 was powered by the BMW 801 C-2 and the A-3 by the more powerful BMW 801 D-1. The Fw 190 was now

delivered to units other than JG 26. JG 2 *Richthofen*, JG 1 *Oesau* and JG 5, the *Eismeergeschwader* (Polar Sea Wing), were all issued the new Fw 190 A-2. By the time production of the two variants ended in December 1942, a total of 933 machines had been delivered by Focke-Wulf and the licensed manufacturers, Fieseler, AGO and Arado. The Fw 190 A-3 was issued to JG 1, JG 2, JG 5, JG 26, JG 51 and to two close-support units, SG 1 and SG 2.

Fw 190 A-1 and a Do 217 E.

A Fw 190 A-1 at Bordeaux-Merignac. Behind it is a Do 217 E of KG 40.

A-1/U1 WNr. 006.

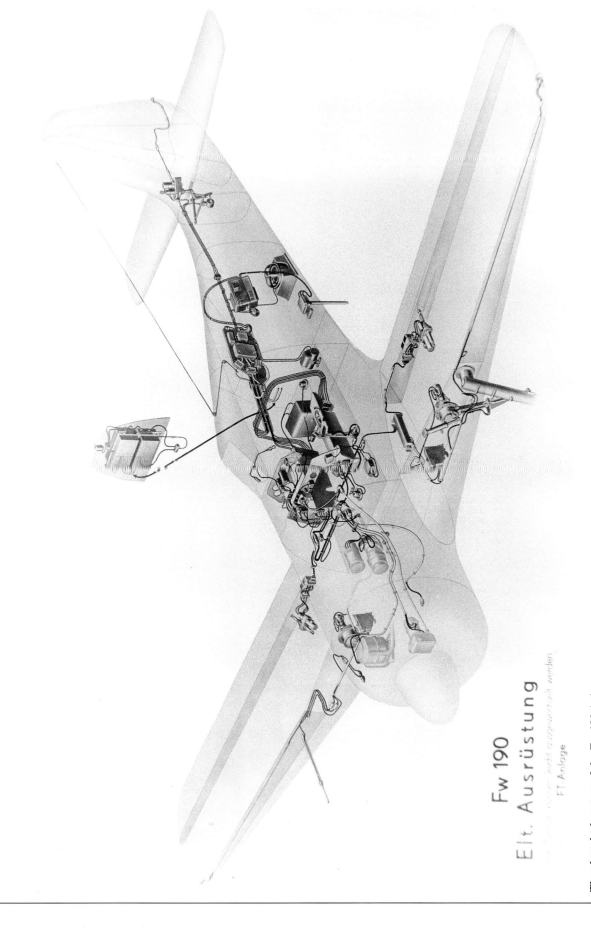

Fw 190
Elt. Ausrüstung

FT Anlage

The electrical system of the Fw 190 A-1.

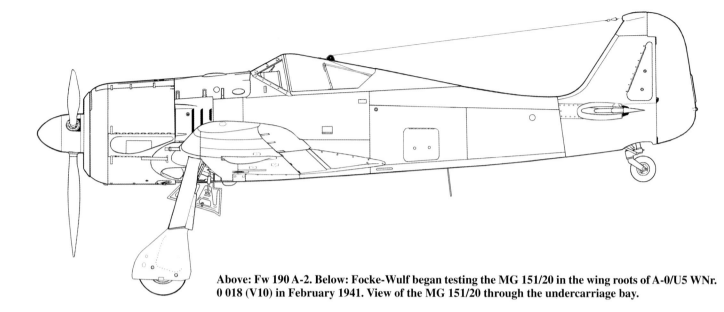

Above: Fw 190 A-2. Below: Focke-Wulf began testing the MG 151/20 in the wing roots of A-0/U5 WNr. 0 018 (V10) in February 1941. View of the MG 151/20 through the undercarriage bay.

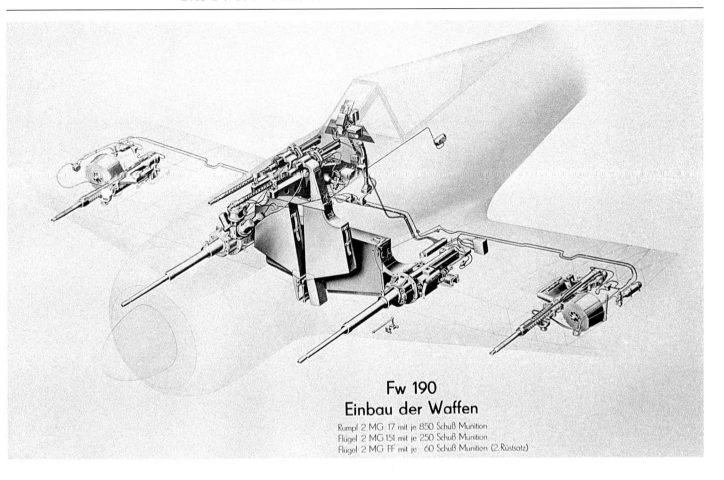

Fw 190
Einbau der Waffen

Rumpf 2 MG 17 mit je 850 Schuß Munition
Flügel 2 MG 151 mit je 250 Schuß Munition
Flügel 2 MG FF mit je 60 Schuß Munition (2. Rüstsatz)

Above: This drawing illustrates the revised armament package consisting of two fuselage-mounted MG 17 machine-guns, two MG 151 cannon in the wing roots and two MG FF cannon in the outer wings. Right: Fw 190 A-2 under construction. The MG 151 cannon have been installed in WNr. 121. The main undercarriage was modified from that of the A-1.

Fw 19o A-2 mit BMW 8o1 C zw. D
=================================
Zeichnung Nr. 19o.oo-168

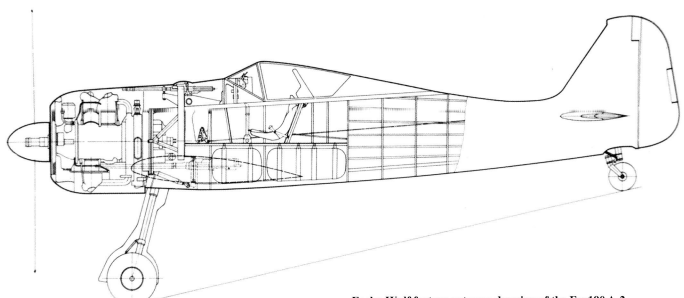

Focke-Wulf factory cutaway drawing of the Fw 190 A-2.

The Fw 190 was capable of carrying up to 500 kg of bombs beneath the fuselage. The success of the Fw 190 in the close-support role soon led to the F-series, which was optimized for that role. A number of production Fw 190 A-3s were used for test purposes. One of these was the Fw 190 A-3/U1, *Werknummer* 270. The aircraft's engine was moved forward, lengthening the fuselage ahead of the wing roots.

Werknummer 386 was fitted with firing tubes for RZ 65 rockets in the outer wings. The RZ 65 was developed as a means for fighters to engage enemy bombers from beyond the range of their defensive weapons. It was also planned to use the RZ 65 against surface targets. The RZ 65 was tested with both the Fw 190 A-3 and the Bf 109 F-2. Mass production of the RZ 65 was never begun, however, and the A-3/U2 remained

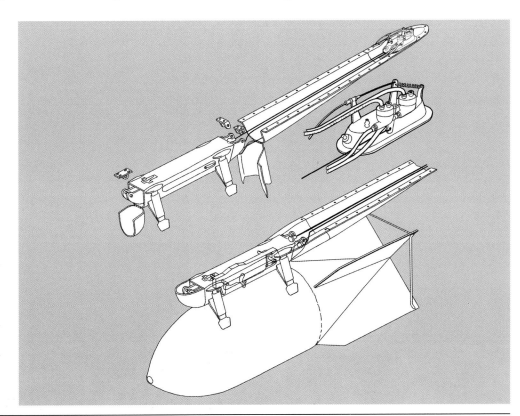

Facing page:
Top: This photo shows the location of the MG 151/20 cannon in the left wing root. On the right is the main spar, left the landing flap.
Bottom: Open access panel on the undersurface of the wing of the Fw 190 A-2 which provided access to the outer wing weapons.

Right: Ventral bomb rack with electric release mechanism.

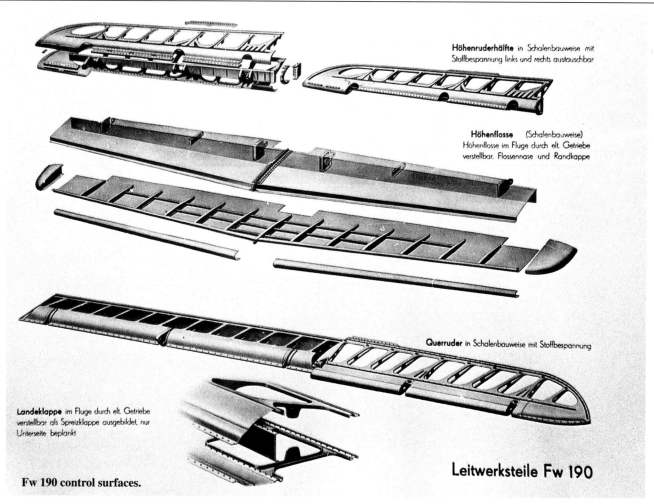

Höhenruderhälfte in Schalenbauweise mit Stoffbespannung links und rechts austauschbar

Höhenflosse (Schalenbauweise) Höhenflosse im Fluge durch elt. Getriebe verstellbar. Flossennase und Randkappe

Querruder in Schalenbauweise mit Stoffbespannung

Landeklappe im Fluge durch elt. Getriebe verstellbar als Spreizklappe ausgebildet, nur Unterseite beplankt

Leitwerksteile Fw 190

Fw 190 control surfaces.

A-2 landing flap with position indicator.

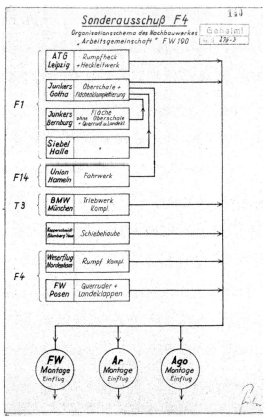

Mass production of the Fw 190 made it necessary to completely reorganize the production facilities and subcontractors. The table on the left clearly depicts this working group. Final assembly was done by Focke-Wulf in Bremen, Arado in Warnemünde and AGO in Oschersleben.

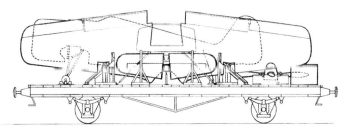

Bahntransport Fw 190

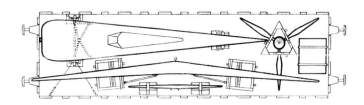

The loading and transport of a complete aircraft was tested using A-0 WNr. 0 009 and a flatbed car.

Type Sheet Fw 190 A-2

Type	Fw 190
Wing area	18.3 m²
Wingspan	10.50 m
Maximum height	3.95 m
Maximum length	8.65 m
Power plant	BMW 801 D
Takeoff power	1,700 h.p. at 2,700 rpm at 0 m
	1,450 h.p. at 2,700 rpm at 5700 m
Propeller revolutions	1,290 rpm
Propeller	3-blade metal variable-pitch, D = 3.3 m

Performance at a Gross Weight of 3850 kg

Maximum speed at takeoff and emergency power at height of

0 m	560 km/h
1500 m	602 km/h
3500 m	602 km/h
6700 m	700 km/h
8000 m	685 km/h
10000 m	650 km/6

Speed at climb and combat power at height of

0 m	532 km/h
1600 m	575 km/h
3200 m	575 km/h
6200 m	660 km/h
8000 m	638 km/h
10000 m	602 km/h

Rate of climb at ground level		17 m/sec
Time to climb to	2000 m	2.1 min
	4000 m	4.5 min
	6000 m	7.2 min
	8000 m	10 min
	10000 m	16.1 min
Service ceiling		11800 m
Takeoff distance		300 m
Landing speed		130 km/h
Range	at 5000 m	750 km

Additional Technical Information on the Fw 190 A-2

Undercarriage wheel track	3500 mm
Wheel diameter Main undercarriage	700 x 175 mm
Electro-mechanically operated	
Tailwheel	350 x 135 mm
Electro-mechanically operated	
Gross weight	3850 kg in fighter role with 2 MG 17 and 2 MG 151
Fuel	524 liters (232 l in front tank, 292 liters in rear tank)
Oil	42 liters (max. 55 liters)
Power Plant	14-cylinder BMW 801 D air-cooled twin-row radial

This excellent photograph illustrates how well the designers of the Fw 190 succeeded in mating the bulky radial engine and machine-gun armament with the forward fuselage. The high standard of workmanship is evident.

Cockpit of the Fw 190 A-2

1	Left console
2	Throttle lever and propeller pitch control
3	Emergency undercarriage lowering handle
4	Fine and coarse altimeter
5	Engine starter brushes withdrawal button
6	Shut-off valve lever
7	FuG 16
8	Panel lighting dimmer switch
9	FuG 25
10	Boost pressure gauge
11	Propeller pitch indicator
12	Fuel contents gauge
13	Fuel contents gauge selector switch
14	Cooling flap hand crank
15	Fuel and oil pressure gauge
16	Oil temperature gauge
17	SUM AP 20 starter pump

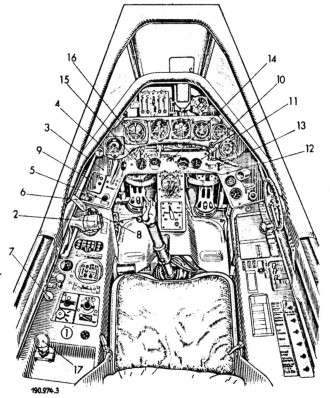

Facing page:
Top: The main instrument panel of the A-2. Bottom: The right console.

Below: The left console of the A-2.

WNr. 121, à Fw 190 A-2, is refueled on the Bremen airfield.

Fw 190 A-2, WNr. 222, manufacturer's code KE+XY,
undergoes a close inspection.

Above: *Werknummer* **226, a Fw 190 A-2 production aircraft; behind it is WNr. 096, an A-1/U1. Below: WNr. 433, a Fw 190 A-2, nearing completion. In the background is WNr. 432.**

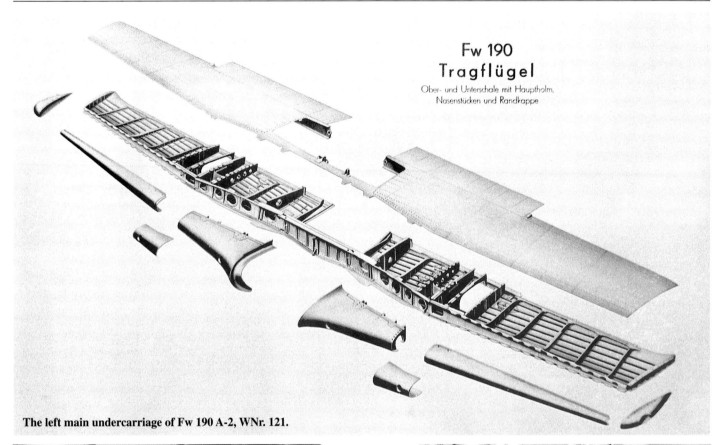

Fw 190
Tragflügel
Ober- und Unterschale mit Hauptholm,
Nasenstücken und Randkappe

The left main undercarriage of Fw 190 A-2, WNr. 121.

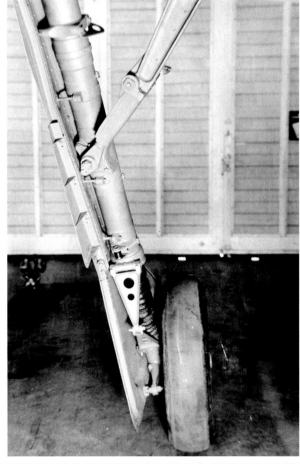

Main undercarriage of the A-2.

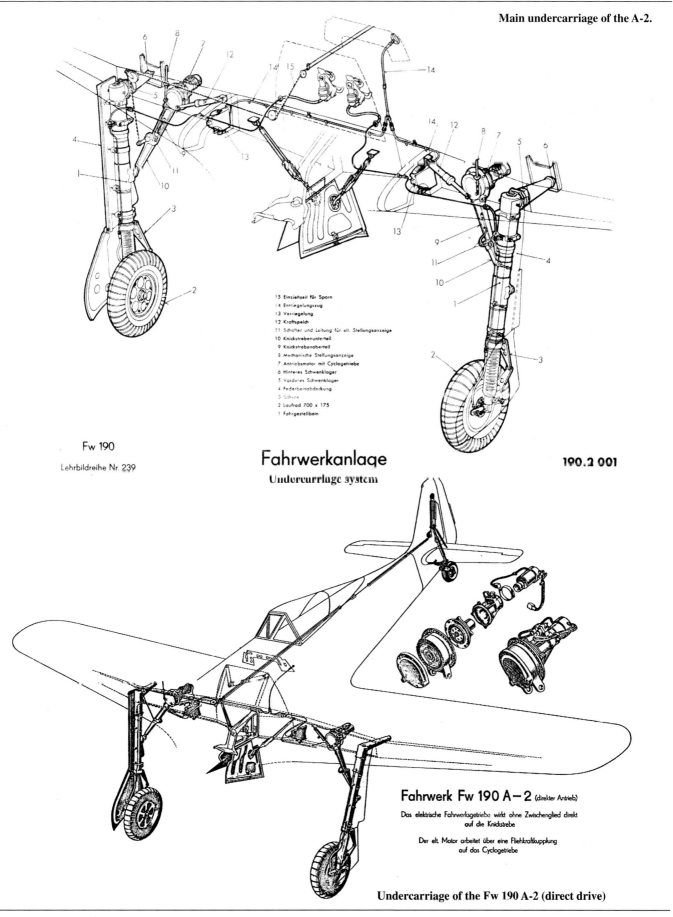

15 Einziehseil für Sporn
14 Entriegelungszug
13 Verriegelung
12 Kraftspeich
11 Schalter und Leitung für elt. Stellungsanzeige
10 Knickstrebenunterteil
9 Knickstrebenoberteil
8 Mechanische Stellungsanzeige
7 Antriebsmotor mit Cyclogetriebe
6 Hinteres Schwenklager
5 Vorderes Schwenklager
4 Federbeinabdeckung
3 Schere
2 Laufrad 700 x 175
1 Fahrgestellbein

Fw 190

Lehrbildreihe Nr. 239

Fahrwerkanlage
Undercarriage system

190.2 001

Fahrwerk Fw 190 A–2 (direkter Antrieb)

Das elektrische Fahrwerksgetriebe wirkt ohne Zwischenglied direkt
auf die Knickstrebe

Der elt. Motor arbeitet über eine Fliehkraftkupplung
auf das Cyclogetriebe

Undercarriage of the Fw 190 A-2 (direct drive)

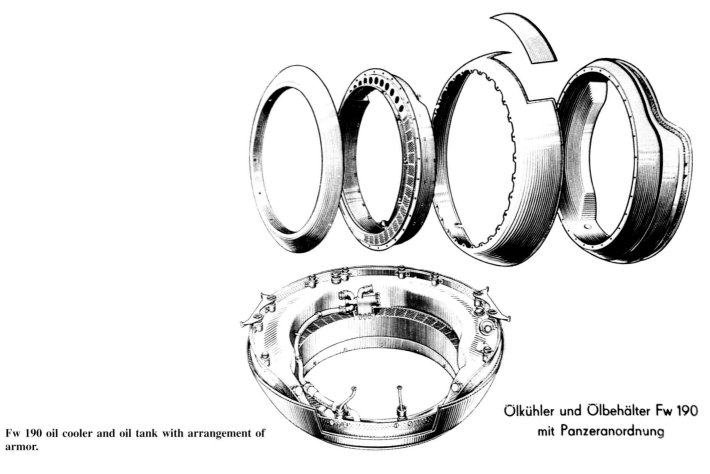

Fw 190 oil cooler and oil tank with arrangement of armor.

Ölkühler und Ölbehälter Fw 190 mit Panzeranordnung

a one-off. The Fw 190 A-3/U3 (WNr. 300) was used to test the aircraft in the reconnaissance role. A small batch of twelve Fw 190 A-3/U4 reconnaissance aircraft was built. Production was completed by November 1942. With a gross weight of 3900 kg, the reconnaissance version was capable of reaching 662 km/h at a height of 6200 meters. A dedicated reconnaissance version, the Fw 190 E-1, was supposed to have entered production in June 1943.

Facing page, bottom:
This A-2, WNr. 346, was completed by Focke-Wulf in Bremen at the beginning of 1942. "Black 14" was flown by 8./JG 2.

This photograph of Fw 190 A-2, WNr. 232, was taken in France in May 1942. The pilot of "Yellow 2" was Ludwig Hartmann of 9./JG 2.

"Yellow 1," a Fw 190 A-2 with the WNr. 0 120 228, was operated by 9./JG 2.

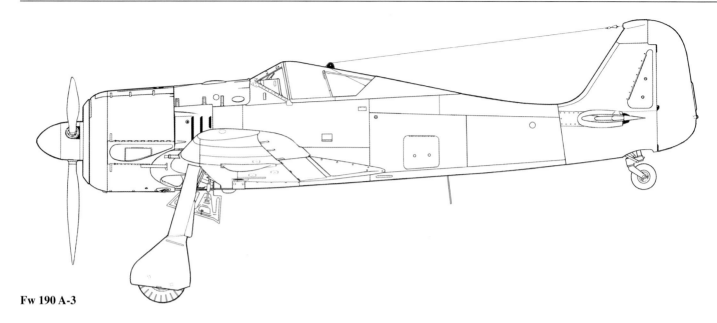

Fw 190 A-3

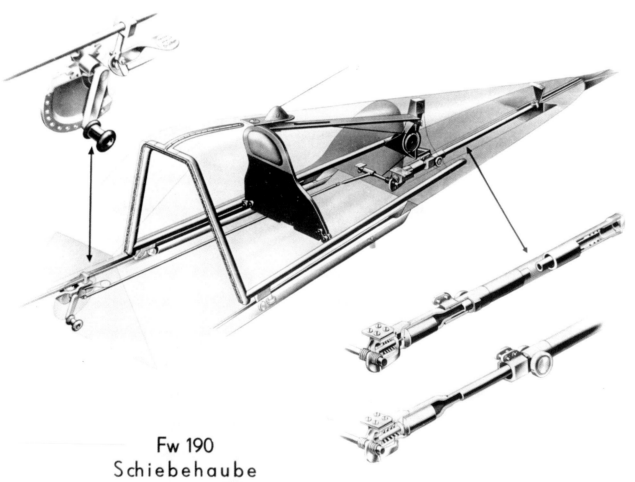

Fw 190
Schiebehaube

Durch Niederschlagen des Auslösehebels 1 wird die
Auslösestange 2 ausgekuppelt und der Schlagbolzen 3 für die
Druckpatrone 4 freigegeben.

The sliding canopy as fitted to the Fw 190 A-2 to A-6.

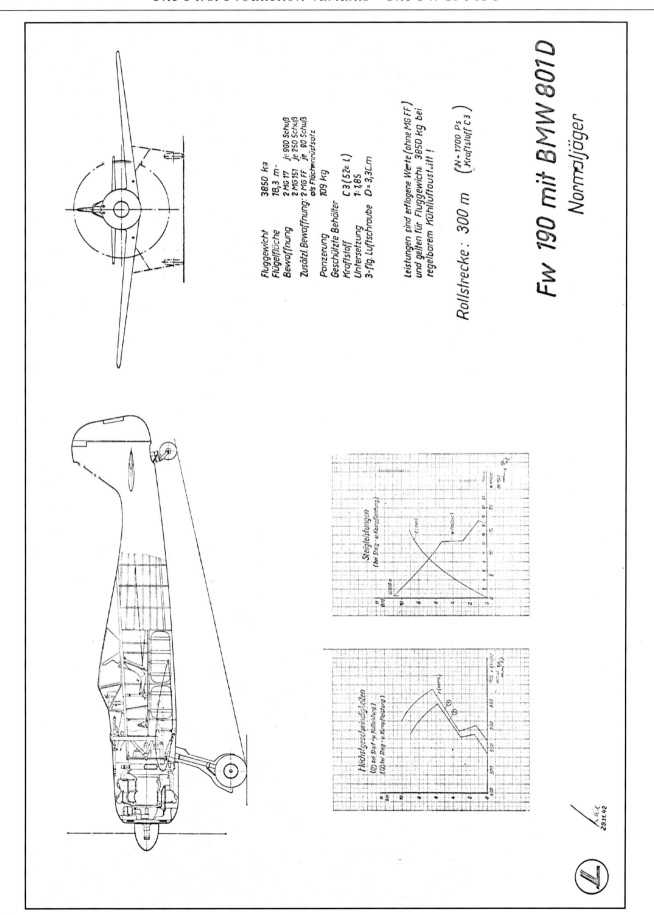

Fw 190 mit BMW 801D

Normaljäger

Rollstrecke: 300 m   (N = 1700 Ps
Kraftstoff C 3)

Fluggewicht   3850 kg
Flügelfläche   18,3 m²
Bewaffnung   2 MG 17   je 900 Schuß
Zusätzl.Bewaffnung: 2 MG 151   je 250 Schuß
                     2 MG FF   je 90 Schuß
                     als Flächeneinsatz
Panzerung   109 kg
Geschützte Behälter
Kraftstoff   C 3 (52 = L)
Untersetzung   1:1,85
3-flg. Luftschraube D = 3,3 m

Leistungen sind erflogene Werte (ohne MG FF)
und gelten für Fluggewicht 3850 kg bei
regelbarem Kühlluftaustritt !

Steigleistungen
(bei Steig- u.Kampfleistung)

Höchstgeschwindigkeiten
① bei Start- u. Notleistung
② bei Steig-v. Kampfleistung

Undercarriage of the Fw 190 A-3. Left WNr. 313, right WNr. 265.

In 1943 test pilot Stein and engineer Rietz of Focke-Wulf were guests of III./ JG 2 in Cherbourg. Knight's Cross wearer Kurt Bühligen is in the center of the photo wearing the life vest. Fw 190 A-3s are parked in the background.

Fw 190 A-3s. On the left is aircraft "3", left "7", both of 8./JG 2. Obfw. Josef Wurmheller, one of the most successful fighter pilots on the Channe in the summer of 1942, flew "White 3".

Fw 190
Einbau der Waffen

Rumpf 2 MG 17 mit je 850 Schuß Munition
Flügel 2 MG 151 mit je 250 Schuß Munition
Flügel 2 MG FF mit je 60 Schuß Munition (2. Rüstsatz)

Armament of the Fw 190 A-3.

Pilot Heinz Hanke of I./JG 1 with his Fw 190 A-3.

Factory photo of Fw 190 A-3, WNr. 463.

A series of propaganda photos intended to convey an impression of Luftwaffe operations over the English Channel in 1942.

I Flew the 190

Memories of Eberhard Geyer, Fighter and Ferry Pilot

Eberhard Geyer was born on 17 September 1922. Gliding was a lifelong passion, and in September 1940 he found employment with Schempp-Hirth, builders of gliders.

Two years later, he and chief engineer Hubert Clompe formed Schempp-Hirth's test-flying section. Geyer subse-

quently volunteered for pilot training, and in April 1942 he was assigned to a flight training regiment in Kaufbeuren.

At that time the training of pilots by the Luftwaffe was not a matter of particular urgency. As a result, Geyer did not arrive at the fighter pre-school in Magdeburg-South until

Eberhard Geyer, strapped into the Gö 3 "Minimax," and Hubert Clompe (left).

Above and Facing page: Eberhard Geyer as a Luftwaffe glider pilot.

February 1944. There he trained on the He 51 and the Fw 56 Stösser. Afterwards he was required to complete two flights in the Ar 96 at A/B School 102 in Zerbst. A short time later he began the Fw 190 A-4 ground school in Hildesheim, where each pilot subsequently made four flights in the aircraft. In September 1944 Eberhard Geyer began making ferry flights for the Luftwaffe.

"I remember one of my first ferry flights in the A-4. My destination was a forward airfield in Westphalia. It was late afternoon and there were many enemy aircraft about that day. When I flew over the airfield, they fired two red flares, the signal to pull up and go around. I circled around and approached the field again. When I looked behind, I saw a fighter with a big radial engine on my tail. I immediately thought it was a Thunderbolt. We circled the airfield in a tight turn at a height of 200 to 250 meters. Below me I saw a quadruple anti-aircraft gun and hoped that the gunners would shoot down the Thunderbolt. We turned very, very tightly. If one stalled the A-4 in a tight turn, it rolled in the opposite direction. If one waited for it, it was possible to make a beautiful half roll and dive and fly away in the opposite direction. When I did this, I could see the other pilot and his machine. The aircraft behind me was a Fw 190. I then climbed up and made a reversal, which placed me directly behind him. After landing and handing over the aircraft, a Leutnant came over to me and said, `Obergefreiter, were you the pilot just then?' I replied that I was, and he said to me, `You did that very nicely, getting behind me'.

While on another ferry flight to Westphalia, abeam the Hermann Monument I saw a seriously-damaged heavy bomber with two engines out. The B-24 was flying very slowly and I quickly overtook it. I was thinking about attacking the B-24, when suddenly I saw tracers flashing past my 190. Two

The Focke-Wulf Fw 56 A "Stösser." This mixed-construction aircraft was conceived by Mittelhuber, while Rudolf Blaser was responsible for the design work. Kurt Tank tested the Fw 56 in 1934. The Fw 56 reached a maximum of 270 km/h at low level, while maximum allowable diving speed was 480 km/h. It was used to train fighter and dive bomber pilots until the end of the war.

Mustangs were turning in behind me. I immediately climbed up into a cloud bank. When I came out on top, the two Mustangs were still behind me. I then dove back into the cloud and switched on the artificial horizon. After about 20 minutes I flew out again and the Mustangs were nowhere to be seen. Later, when I handed the 190 over at the airfield, the DF loop was missing. It was well that I had pulled up as soon as I was attacked, as their bullets merely struck my DF loop.

The first Fw 190 D-9s arrived in Zerbst at the end of October 1944. I had already attended the D-9 ground school, once again in Hildesheim, in September. The D-9 flew like a dream. Application of full throttle resulted in a stiff jolt in the back. Once 300 km/h had been reached, it was possible to climb the D-9 at a 45 degree angle to 3000 meters with no loss in speed. That was fantastic. I believe that the D-9 turned less well than the A-4, however we never had the opportunity to find out. Our first ferry flight was at the end of October, when we were to deliver a flight of four to Reinsehlen. A *Gruppe* of JG 54 was based there. Although visibility had been forecast to be unlimited, the weather was visibly worsening. We flew straight into a layer of cloud. Our flight leader, a veteran bomber pilot, broke up the formation and merely instructed us to climb up through the cloud. I saw a railway line below me and flew back along it to an airfield I had seen earlier. There was nothing to be seen of the other three machines. I made my approach to the airfield, but in spite of several attempts my port undercarriage leg refused to come down. I still had a 300-liter auxiliary tank beneath me and I obviously wanted to avoid a belly landing. I jettisoned the tank away from the airfield and flew back. When I turned on final I saw that the port undercarriage leg was now down. What luck. I was forced to wait on the ground for three days until the fog lifted, then I flew my D-9 to Reinsehlen.

I was the only member of the formation to deliver his aircraft. A short time later I learned that the veteran bomber pilot had been able to fly his D-9 back to Zerbst, while the other two pilots flew their D-9s into the ground. One pilot died, the other was severely injured.

At the beginning of January 1945 I was tasked to ferry a Fw 190 to JG 1 in Twenthe, Holland.

Fw 190 A-1, WNr. 967, manufacturer's code TI+DQ. This aircraft was later operated by the 4. Staffel of JG 26.

Fw 190 A-3, WNr. 503.

It was after 'Operation *Bodenplatte*', and the unit's *I. Gruppe* was making preparations to transfer to the east. The *Gruppe* took off too late, however. The staff flight and the *1. Staffel* got away safely, but then the *2.* and *3. Staffel* were jumped by Spitfires, and ten to twelve machines were shot down. After this disaster the *Gruppe* immediately ordered me to remain and sent a telex requesting my papers. From that time on I was a member of the *1. Staffel* of JG 1. On the evening of 14 January we took off for Werneuchen, planning to fly on to Insterburg the following day. Then I was sent back to Twenthe to collect a 190 that had been left behind. I flew to Holp in a Siebel 204 and then proceeded to Magdeburg by rail. Magdeburg had been heavily bombed the night before, and I was forced to walk twelve kilometers through the city carrying my parachute, literally stepping over bodies. It was a frightful sight. I collected the 190 at Twenthe and took off after dark. On the way back I stopped in Stettin. There I handed the 190 over to the maintenance people so that it could be painted in winter camouflage (white with gray stripes) overnight. The situation at the front was uncertain. No one knew exactly where I./JG 1 was, therefore I was ordered to first fly to Danzig-Langfuhr.

As I approached the airfield, I was greeted by a red flare. Danzig was already under fire. I broke off my approach and headed toward the Baltic. I raised my undercarriage and tried to increase power, but my engine control system was no longer functioning.

The engine remained throttled back, producing insufficient power to maintain height. I flew into solid white cloud of snow at a height of 150 meters. I jettisoned the canopy and came down in the snow. The 190 bounced twice and came to a stop. I immediately climbed out onto the left wing. Lying next to me on the ground was a playing card, the seven of diamonds. I took it with me. I had been extremely luck. Beside the 190 on the right was an 88-mm anti-aircraft gun, to the left a high wall surrounding a cemetery.

I approached the local military commander in an effort to get back somehow. The only possibility was to hitch a ride on an aircraft evacuating wounded to Stolp. The machine was completely overloaded and smelled terrible. As we ap-

Three new Fw 190 A-3s have been delivered to an operational unit. The two aircraft in the rear still wear the factory finish.

proached, I saw four Fw 190s parked at the edge of the airfield.

After landing I went to the local commander and asked whom the Fw 190s belonged to. I was told that the four Fw 190s had been parked there the previous autumn. With the help of a mechanic and a Kettenkrad, I towed one Fw 190 back to the airfield. I let the engine warm up, as I had no way of knowing if the aircraft was equipped for cold starts. Soon after departure, at a height of 250 meters, the engine began to run rough. I retracted the flaps and undercarriage and made a 180 degree turn. Soon afterwards the engine quit. I managed to get the undercarriage down at the last minute and came to a stop under the wing of a Ju 52. I stuck a stick into the oil and found sand on the end—sabotage! I had the oil drained from the next Fw 190 and refilled. From the military commander I learned that my *Gruppe* was in Swinemünde auf Usedom. I arrived there, but a few days later we had to hand over all available Fw 190s to the *II.* and *III. Gruppe* and then proceed to Parchim. From Parchim we then proceeded to Warnemünde. There we were briefed by Heinkel on the new

Volksjäger (People's Fighter). In the morning we learned more about the He 162 from Heinkel test pilots. Our *Gruppe* was to receive prototypes straight from the factory. Ten days later we returned to Parchim. We had to wait another week before the first three *Volksjäger* arrived. With these three He 162s we began flying. One aircraft was lost to us as a result of a curious sentry. During the night he climbed into the cockpit and began playing with the levers. The He 162 had the first ejector seat we had seen. The man fired himself through the roof of the hangar. He was not seriously hurt, but the He 162 was rendered unserviceable. This left us with just two serviceable aircraft for training. I was waiting for my turn to fly a circuit and watched as an Unteroffizier took off. He pulled the throttle back too far while on approach and the engine quit. He had not lowered the undercarriage, and the aircraft swooped across the Eider and landed in some bushes. He broke several vertebra in the landing. This left us with just one He 162. In the days that followed, we were carpet-bombed from morning to evening and the airfield was attacked by fighter-bombers. When the attacks ended, there was little left. The

The Fw 190 D-9/R5 with ETC 71 bomb racks beneath the wings was used as a close-support aircraft. Powered by a Jumo 213 A-1 engine developing 1,770 h.p., the aircraft had a maximum speed of 686 km/h at a height of 6600 m.

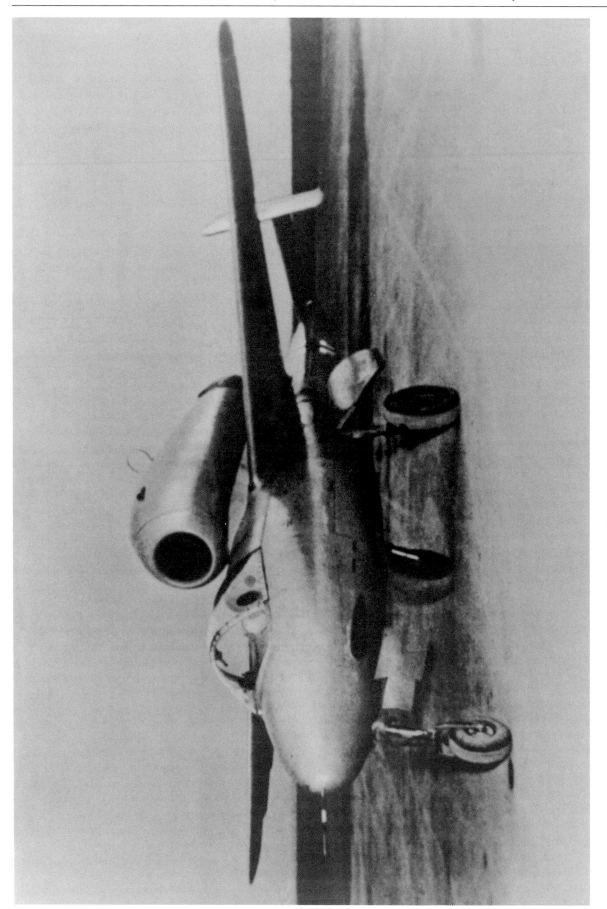

Like the Me 262, the He 162 Volksjäger could only be flown by experienced pilots.

A Fw 190 A-4 on an eastern front airfield. The robust design of the Fw 190 proved an asset in the primitive conditions encountered in the east.

Fw 190 A-3 in the air.

only remaining He 162 had been destroyed on the ground. Normal flying activities were impossible. Following this, groups of pilots were assembled in Parchim for assignment to other units. The group I was in was supposed to join JG 52. We traveled by rail to Schweidnitz, southwest of Breslau, where III./JG 52 was based. At that time the *Gruppe* was flying supply missions over the Breslau Pocket, mainly dropping munitions. I and two other pilots received a few days of theoretical training, as none of us had flown the 109 Gustav before. Afterwards we flew circuits in the 109. After completing four circuits we were checked out on the 109.

At the end of April 45 we flew to Cottbus in a Siebel 204 to collect five new 109s. Immediately after landing each of us selected one of the parked aircraft. During takeoff I noticed a problem with the 109's brakes. When I landed, the brakes failed completely and the 109 swung to the left. In vain, I tried to straighten it out by applying full opposite rudder. There was nothing I could do. At that time we were sharing the airfield with a close-support unit. I found myself heading straight toward four Fw 190 close-support aircraft already armed with bombs beneath their wings. My propeller struck the wing of the first Fw 190 and my right undercarriage leg collapsed. My last landing for the *Luftwaffe* resulted in two German aircraft destroyed on the ground. A few days later the war was over."

The Multipurpose Fighter

With the entry into service of the improved Fw 190 A-3, the Focke-Wulf Fw 190 had firmly established itself as a fighter aircraft. The most important factor in this was the improved reliability of the BMW 801 D-2 engine and its increased power over the BMW 801 C.

The BMW 801 D-2's increased performance was achieved by increasing compression (1:7.5 instead of 1:6.5) and rais-ing the gear ratios of the two supercharger speeds. The engine also required C3 fuel.

In this configuration the BMW 801 D-2 produced 1,770 h.p. for takeoff at 2,700 rpm and 1.42 atm of boost. This enabled the Fw 190 A-3 to achieve 564 km/h at ground level and a top speed of 680 km/h at a height of 6500 meters. The English response to the superiority of the Fw 190 A-3 was

In-flight photo of A-3, WNr. 471.

Factory photo of Fw 190 A-3, WNr. 471.

Type Sheet Fw 190 A-3

Type	Fw 190
Wing area	18.3 m²
Wingspan	10.50 m
Maximum height	3.95 m
Maximum length	8.65 m
Power plant	BMW 801 D2
Takeoff power	1,700 h.p. at 2,700 rpm at 0 m
	C3 / 97 Octane Fuel
Propeller revolutions	1,290 rpm
Propeller	3-blade metal variable-pitch, D = 3.3 m

Performance at a Gross Weight of 3850 kg

Maximum speed at takeoff and emergency power at height of

	0 m	565 km/h
	1300 m	600 km/h
	3200 m	585 km/h
	6500 m	680 km/h
	8000 m	660 km/h
	10000 m	610 km/6
Rate of climb at ground level	16.5 m/sec	
Time to climb to	2000 m	2.0 min
	4000 m	4.6 min
	6000 m	7.2 min
	8000 m	11.3 min
	9000 m	15.0 min
Service ceiling		11000 m
Takeoff distance		300 m
Landing speed		130 km/h
Range at cruise power at 5000 m		810 km

Additional Technical Information on the Fw 190 A-3

Undercarriage wheel track	3500 mm
Wheel diameter Main undercarriage	700 x 175 mm
Electro-mechanically operated	
Tailwheel	350 x 135 mm
Electro-mechanically operated	
Fuel	524 liters (232 l in front tank, 292 liters in rear tank)
Oil	42 liters (max. 55 liters)
Power Plant	14-cylinder BMW 801 D-2 air-cooled twin-row radial

the improved Spitfire Mk.IX, powered by a Rolls Royce Merlin 66 producing 1,680 h.p. The Spitfire Mk.IX enabled the RAF to achieve a level of parity with the potent Fw 190. Whereas the earlier Spitfire Mk.V had been clearly inferior, there was little to choose between the new Spitfire and the Fw 190 at altitudes up to 6700 meters. The English had wiped out the technical advantage enjoyed by the Germans, and it was obvious that they would try to further improve the performance of the Spitfire.

The German side did not stand still, however. While Focke-Wulf made changes to the Fw 190's airframe, BMW worked to further improve the BMW 801 engine. It was hoped that the BMW 801 F would produce another significant increase in performance. The second objective was to rationalize the production of components. Although the 2,000 h.p. BMW 801 E was ready for production, shortages of machine tools meant that production never fully got under way. Toward the end of the war a hybrid was produced by combining components of the BMW 801 D and E engines.

Fw 190 A-3, WNr. 471.

Fw 190 A   Geheim!

	Verwendung	Musterprüfung	Abnehmer	Werk-Nr.	Triebwerk	Rumpf	Flügel i.	Flügel a.	Rumpf	Fläche	Bildgeräte	FT-Anlage	Bemerkungen	Bezchng.	Stck.	Auslieferg.
						Schußwaffe			**Abwurfw./Zusatzbeh.**						**Flugzeuge**	
A-3	Jäger	V14	RLM	190.0130 bis 560	BMW 801 D	2 MG 17	2 MG 151	(2 MG FF)	(500 kg)(250 kg)(300 ltr)			FuG VII FuG 25		Jäger	siehe A2	8.41÷12.42
A-3/U-1	Jäger/Jäger	V14	RLM	190.0130 270	"	"	"	"	"			"	Musterflugzeug Vorverlegter Motor	"		
A-3/U-2	Jäger/Jäger	V14	RLM	190.0130 386	"	"	"	RZ-65	"			"	Waffenträger RZ-65 Erprobung	"		
A-3/U-3	Aufklärer/Jäger	V14	RLM	190.0130 300	"	"	"	(2 MG FF)	"		(RB 50/30)(RB 75/30)	"	Versuchsträger f. Bildgerät	Aufklärer		
A-3/U-4	Auf-klärer/Höhen-jäger	V14	RLM		"	"	"	—	"		2 RB 12,5/7×9 1 Robot	FuG 17 FuG 25	Robot in Flächennase links	Aufklärer „H"	12	
A-3/U-7	Höhen-jäger	V14	RLM	528,3031	"	—	"	(2 MG FF)	"			FuG VII FuG 25	Erleichterte Ausführung	1.Höhenjäger		
Aa-3		V14/K3			"	2 MG 17	2 MG 17	2 MG FF				FuG VIIa		„Hamburg"		

The result of the search for increased performance was the Fw 190 A-4, which was capable of using the GM 1 power-boosting system for improved performance. To test improvements and the effectiveness of the GM 1 system, a standard Fw 190 with the *Werknummer* 140 561 was taken from the production line and converted to become the Fw 190 V24.

GM 1 used a liquid oxidizer, which was injected into the engine. This significantly improved combustion at higher altitudes. The system consisted of an injection system and a total of six pressure bottles. Another improvement introduced by this series was provision for tropical equipment. The Fw 190 A-4/trop was identified by its external air intakes with sand filters.

The most obvious external identifying feature of the Fw 190 A-4 was the triangular antenna mast atop the vertical stabilizer for the FuG 16 Z radio.

In addition to offering increased performance, the Fw 190 A-4 also served as the basis for numerous variants intended for roles other than day fighter. The planned Fw 190 A-4/U3 became the Fw 190 F-1, the first close-support variant of the Fw 190, while the Fw 190 A-4/U8 became the Fw 190 G-1, the first fighter-bomber variant.

Fw 190 A-3/U1: the prototype for the later A-5 with lengthened forward fuselage. It also served as prototype for the Fw 190 G-3 fighter-bomber with underwing bomb racks. Manufacturer's code was PG+GY.

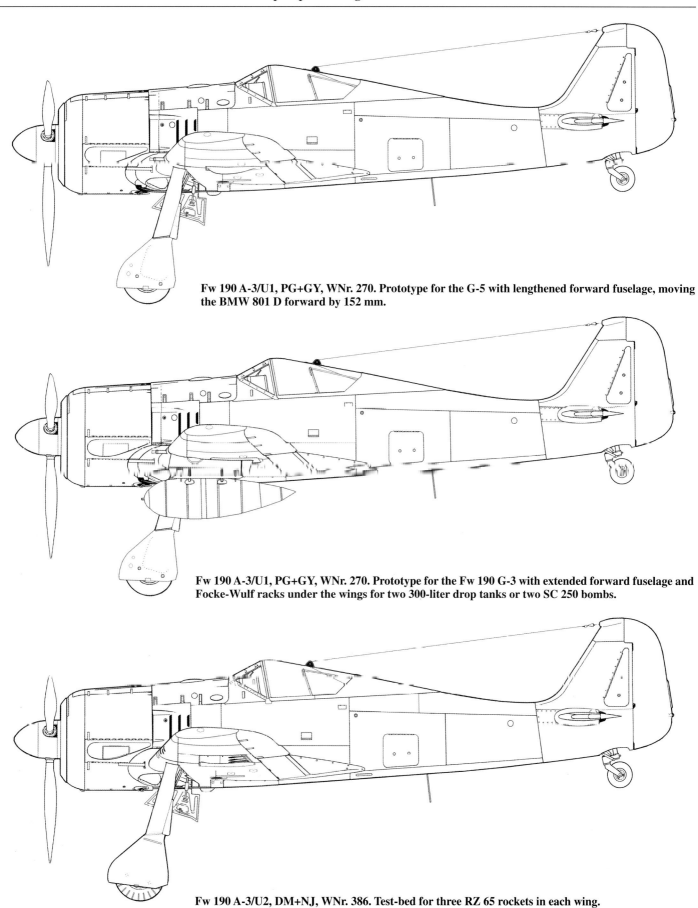

Fw 190 A-3/U1, PG+GY, WNr. 270. Prototype for the G-5 with lengthened forward fuselage, moving the BMW 801 D forward by 152 mm.

Fw 190 A-3/U1, PG+GY, WNr. 270. Prototype for the Fw 190 G-3 with extended forward fuselage and Focke-Wulf racks under the wings for two 300-liter drop tanks or two SC 250 bombs.

Fw 190 A-3/U2, DM+NJ, WNr. 386. Test-bed for three RZ 65 rockets in each wing.

Fw 190 A-3/U3: installation in the fuselage of WNr. 300 for Rb 50x30 or Rb 75x30 cameras.

Fw 190 A-3/U3: system with camera opening closed.

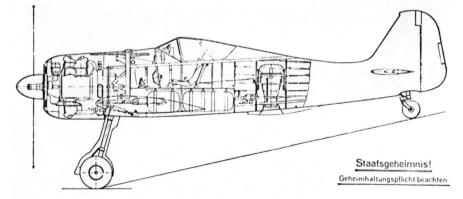

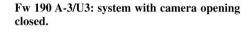

Staatsgeheimnis!
Geheimhaltungspflicht beachten.

Fw 190 Aufklärer

Musterflugzeuge   A-3/U-4   Nov. 1942
vorläufige Serienflugzeuge A-5/U-4 ab Jan.1943
endgültige Serienflugzeuge E-1   ab Juni 1943

14.12.42

The Fw 190 A-3/U3, WNr. 300, was the test-bed for a camera-equipped reconnaissance version.

The Fw 190 A-3/U4: Aufklärer H (Reconnaissance Aircraft H), with two 12.5 cameras in the fuselage and a cine camera in the port wing (7x9). A ventral bomb rack was also planned.

Fw 190 A-3/U3: experimental installation of a large camera in the fuselage of WNr. 300.

Fw 190 A-3/U4: Mockup of the EK 16 cine camera in the port wing of WNr. 301.

Fw 190 A-3/U4: Two cameras in the fuselage of the Aufklärer H.

Fw 190 A-3/U4: Fairing on the underside of the fuselage.

Fw 190 A-3 A-3/U4.

The Fw 190 A-4/U4 was used for strategic photo reconnaissance missions. Shown here is "Red 4" of 5.(F)/123.

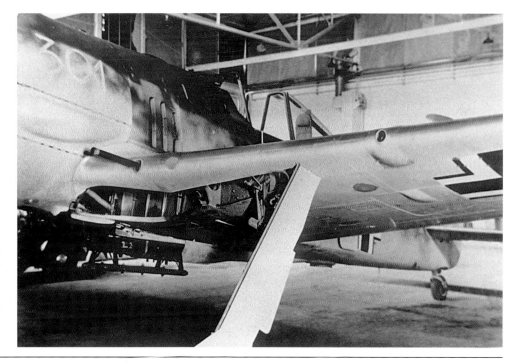

Above right: Overlap control for the Rb50/30 and Rb 75/30 cameras in the cockpit of the Fw 190 A-3/U3, WNr. 300.

Above left: Servicing the cameras of a Fw 190.

Fw 190 A-3/U4, WNr. 301.

Fw 190 A-3/U4, WNr. 447, with ER 4 rack for four 50-kg SC 50 bombs on the fuselage ETC.

While the G-series was developed into so-called *Jabo-Rei*, or long-range fighter-bombers, the F-series represented a new generation of close-support aircraft. Gun armament of the G-series aircraft was reduced to two MG 151 cannon in the wing roots. The G-1 was, however, capable of carrying two 300-liter fuel tanks beneath the outer wings, increasing the Fw 190's radius of action considerably. With two 300-liter fuel tanks and one 500-kg bomb on the fuselage rack, gross weight rose to 4730 kg. This reduced the aircraft's maximum speed to 545 km/h at 6200 meters. Once the aircraft had dropped its bombs and external tanks, maximum speed rose to 620 km/h. Maximum range was 1650 km.

The close-support versions of the Fw 190 were heavily armored. Total weight of the armor was 360 kg, raising gross weight to 4300 kg. Improvements introduced into the A-series were also incorporated into the F/G-series.

In October 1942 deliveries began to Turkey of 72 Fw 190 Aa-3 aircraft. Unit price was 510,000 RM.

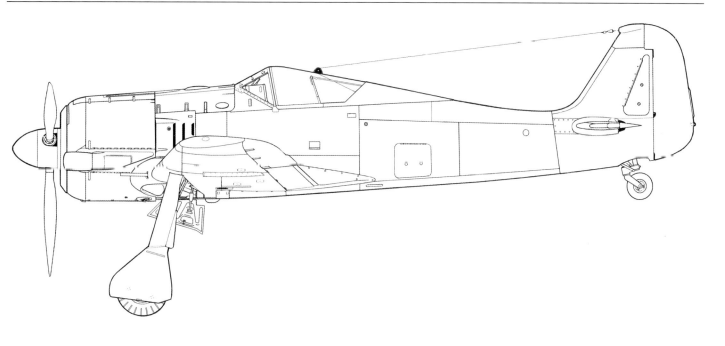

Fw 190 A-3/U7, DC+AB, WNr. 528. It was hoped to improve high altitude performance by decreasing the aircraft's weight. WNr. 530 and 531 were built to this standard as the Höhenjäger 1.

Beginning with the Fw 190 A-5, the engine was moved forward as a result of the steadily-climbing weight of the aircraft. Heavier armament combinations were introduced, in and beneath the outer wings. The two MG FF cannon were replaced by MG 151s. Experimental installations included four MG 151 cannon beneath the wings (*Werknummer* 813 and 814) and two large-caliber MK 103 cannon.

The use of underwing cannon had previously been restricted to the Bf 109. Beginning with the Fw 190 A-6, these were available for installation as armament/equipment sets (*Rüstsätze*).

Focke-Wulf also tested the Fw 190 as a torpedo carrier. A total of three production aircraft (WNr. 871, 872 and 1282) were converted. After acceptance tests by Focke-Wulf test pilots, the aircraft were flown to the Torpedo Weapons Station in Gotenhafen-Hexengrund. In the next chapter Johann Schmitt provides a detailed account of his experiences while flying the Fw 190 torpedo aircraft at Hexengrund.

The Fw 190 Torpedo-Fighter

Memories of Johann Schmitt, Test Pilot with the Hexergrund Torpedo Weapons Station

In October 1942 my Ju 88 was seriously damaged by Spitfires during a mission over Malta. With both engines on fire I was unable to make it to Catania and was forced to crash-land in an orange grove. I was the only survivor. This marked a turning point in my career as a pilot. Following my recovery, in June 1943 I went to Altenburg, where Major Hermann was setting up the "*Wilde Sau*" (Wild Boars), a night fighter unit flying the Me 109 and Fw 190. We carried out night training on the Go 145 and Me 109. One evening we were preparing to take off when an Me 109 approached. When the pilot realized that he was going to land short, he applied throttle. He was unable to compensate for the engine torque, however, and the aircraft rolled over and crashed on the landing cross. The pilot was killed. I didn't much care for this job and I wanted to go back to my old unit. Soon afterwards we moved to Bonn-Hangelar. My comrades had to fly night missions in aircraft of the day fighter units, and many were forced to bail out after running our of fuel. To this day I still do not know who was responsible for me going to the Torpedo Weapons Station in Hexengrund.

On arriving at the Torpedo Weapons Station I made my first acquaintance with the Fw 190. I stood before it in awe, and my pilot's heart began to beat faster. Its appearance made a very solid impression. The wide track undercarriage promised safe landings. Only the massive radial engine detracted from the machine's elegance. There was rather more room in the Fw 190 than the Me 109. The undercarriage also required more attention during takeoff and landing and was altogether rather more sensible. My introduction to the type was trouble-free and I immediately felt at home in the cockpit. While my comrades of the "Wild Boars" had to fly dangerous missions, I was able to cavort about the sky as in peacetime, although test flying did have an element of risk. We had two Fw 190s which we used for test purposes, TD+SI and DZ+LW. We flew the machines hard, especially in testing the TSA-BT. I

Johann Schmitt.

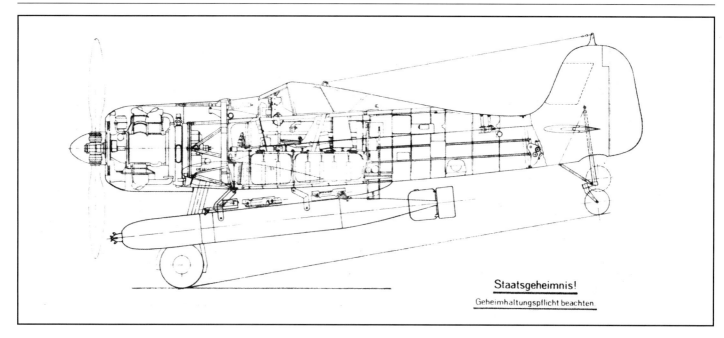

Staatsgeheimnis!

Geheimhaltungspflicht beachten

A-5/U14 cutaway drawing.

flew so-called "BT Tests" in TD+SI with bomb-torpedoes. On these flights we employed the TSA (Low-Altitude Launch System). To carry out the test, we approached in a 45 degree dive, and a computer told us when to make a 6g pullout in order to place the bomb-torpedo in an arc under the keel of a ship. TD+SI had a lengthened tailwheel leg to prevent the fins of the bomb-torpedo from striking the ground during take-off. For landing the tailwheel extended normally. We carried out trials with bomb-torpedoes up to 1400 kg in weight. After some time the 190 went to the maintenance hangar, and I saw with shock how the airframe had suffered.

The two machines mentioned above were later joined by another. Rudolf Heuer, another test pilot with the Torpedo Weapons Station, made a belly landing in the third Fw 190 after a broken connecting rod caused the BMW 801 to give up the ghost. During testing I noted heavy tail unit vibration caused by the high acceleration forces in the dive.

Our engines were somewhat skeptical and called in experts from Focke-Wulf. Focke-Wulf sent a technician, who installed instruments in the baggage compartment behind the seat and connected them with wires to the tail surfaces. He also installed a clear panel. The Focke-Wulf technician

Experimental installation of the ETC 502 for carriage of aerial torpedoes by the Fw 190 A-5/U14.

Fw 190 A-5/U14, WNr. 871, manufacturer's code TD+SI.

WNr. 871 at the Hexengrund torpedo weapons station in northern Germany.

squeezed into the tiny space in the rear—without a parachute. During subsequent test flights he monitored the 190's behavior visually and with his instruments.

I was astonished at the enormous trust the Focke-Wulf employee placed in the Fw 190. Given his unusual seating position, I found this encouraging. After landing he was astonished that the tail section had really fluttered under certain conditions, and he returned to the factory with his findings.

In addition to the bomb-torpedoes, we also tested "normal" aerial torpedoes. To achieve the desired accuracy, the TWP developed the so-called To-Ka-Ge (Torpedo Control Device). If I remember correctly, *Major* Schedt took part in its development. Between the joystick and the firewall there was a box with a control grip on top, which represented the target vessel. While approaching low over the water, one turned this symbol to the exact angle one was viewing the target. This transmitted an impulse to the torpedo. Precision was required in releasing the torpedo, as it could not be al-

lowed to pitch. After release, one had to pull up and fly low over the superstructure of the ship. The Fw 190 did this well. At the time I wondered to myself what the likelihood of being shot down.

Before the Russians came we moved, first to Lübeck-Blankensee and then to the E-Stelle Travemünde. There we continued our tests for a while longer. Toward the end of the war we had a Fw 190 D powered by a Jumo 213 for a short while. I was surprised by how quiet and vibration-free the Jumo 213 was, much different than the BMW 801. Through all the testing I never really cared for the BMW 801. The engine ran roughly and vibrated heavily. Shortly before the end of the war I was supposed to fly a Fw 190 to Veigle in Denmark. However the sky was full of Mosquitoes and nothing came of it. Most of the aircraft were blown up, and the English arrived on 8 May. The Fw 190 was built in Travemünde, and there was a brand new one there.

On 15 May 1945 I was ordered to this machine. A Canadian Captain wanted to fly it to Schwerin. For reasons of

TD+SI with underslung torpedo.

The Fw 190 display in the Hanover-Laatzen Aviation Museum.

safety, I had to demonstrate the Fw 190, which already had British markings. The aircraft had never been flown and was totally out of trim. After two flights I familiarized the Captain with the controls. He gave me a cigarette and I wondered how this man could be my enemy. Then he climbed in and took off. How he got down in Schwerin I do not know; it was a short field. I could never have dreamed that I would be sitting in a Fw 190 again a week after the war. I was proud and sad at the same time.

The Fw 190 Today
New Construction Projects
in Germany

Laatzen Aviation Museum

For the first time there is once again a Fw 190 on public display. The completely new aircraft, which represents a Fw 190 A-8, is on display in the Laatzen Aviation Museum in Hanover and is finished in historically-accurate paint scheme and markings. It is painted in the standard camouflage of mid-1944 and bears the markings of aircraft "Yellow 11" of the 6. *Staffel* of JG 1. The original "Yellow 11", *Werknummer* 170 393, flew from Stoermede in the spring of 1944.

The road leading to the official presentation of the Fw 190 A-8 at the end of 2000 was a long one. The so-called "Project 2000" began eight years earlier. Under the direction of the private museum in Hanover-Laatzen, Günter Leonhardt collection, a search was begun for Fw 190 parts with the goal of completing a Fw 190 by the year 2000.

In the end, original parts recovered from six wrecks were used, but not everything could be taken from original aircraft. The fuselage center section, rudder and wing had to be reproduced by Flug-Werk. The result is a realistic recreation of a Fw 190 A-8 and a visit to the museum is extremely worthwhile.

This G-3 was captured by U.S. forces in North Africa.

This G-3 trop was captured by American forces in North Africa and was used as a training aircraft.

Flug-Werk: Fw 190 A-8/N

To read a book about the Fw 190 is one thing, to see a full scale Fw 190 is another. Every Fw 190 enthusiast in Germany has wished for the opportunity to see a Fw 190 close by and up close. Several examples of the Messerschmitt Bf 109 could be seen in German museums, but there was no Fw 190. Those few Fw 190s which survived the war were taken out of the country. This has now changed. For the first time, there is now a fully flyable Fw 190 in Germany. The aircraft, which bears the designation Fw 190 A-8/N, represents the Fw 190 A-8, which was built in larger numbers than any other variant.

The N stands for *Nachbau*, or reproduction. There is even a new *Werknummer* series, beginning with 990 000. The Fw 190 A-8/N is built by the Flug-Werk GmbH of Gammelsdorf.

Thanks must go to the two owners, Flugkapitän Claus Colling and Dipl.Ing. Günther Wildmoser. The first Fw 190 is to be followed by twelve more, some of them equipped to fly.

Even the need for replacement parts has thought of and these are produced as required. One small disappointment is the power plant. As the BMW 801 is unavailable, the builders have had to turn to the Russian Ash 82 engine.

The first Fw 190 is to be completed by Flug-Werk in 2001. The first flight is planned after the necessary taxiing trials.

The Fw 190 A-8/N reproduction is 450 kg lighter than the original. There is no armor, weapons or ammunition, and the heavy radio equipment of the 1940s is also gone.

Outwardly the A-8/N is 98% identical with the original. Fuel tankage has been increased to 880 liters compared to the 650 liters of the original A-8.

Fw 190 A-8/N in its hangar.

Type Sheet Fw 190 A-8/N

Wing area	18.3 m²	Maximum speed at 6000 m	635 km/h
Wingspan	10.50 m	Cruising speed at 2,300 rpm	585 km/h
Maximum height	3.95 m	Rate of climb	20 m/sec
Length	9.10 m	Landing speed	185 km/h
Power plant	Ash 82 FN	Range	990 km
Volume	42 liters		
Takeoff power	1,900 h.p.	Undercarriage wheel base	3500 mm
Propeller	3-blade metal propeller,	Empty weight	3000 kg
	D = 3.3 m	Gross weight	3600 kg max.
		Fuel	880 liters
		Oil	60 liters

The airframe seen from the right side.

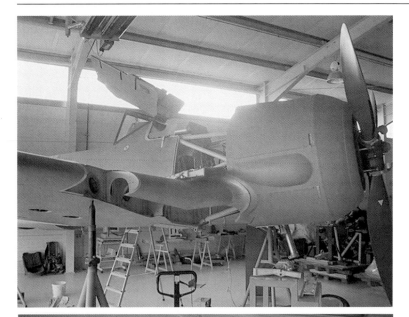